Literacy in Context

TEACHER'S PORTFOLIO

Background notes, information and ideas, plus 48 copymasters for use with the Student's Book

Language of
media and the moving image

John O'Connor

Media consultant   Graham Charlton

General editors   Joan Ward *and* John O'Connor
Literacy consultant   Lyn Ranson
General consultant   Frances Findlay

CAMBRIDGE UNIVERSITY PRESS
www.cambridge.org

ISBN 0-521-80569-4

PUBLISHED BY THE PRESS SYNDICATE OF THE UNIVERSITY OF CAMBRIDGE
The Pitt Building, Trumpington Street, Cambridge, United Kingdom

CAMBRIDGE UNIVERSITY PRESS
The Edinburgh Building, Cambridge CB2 2RU, UK
40 West 20th Street, New York, NY 10011-4211, USA
10 Stamford Road, Oakleigh, VIC 3166, Australia
Ruiz de Alarcón 13, 28014 Madrid, Spain
Dock House, The Waterfront, Cape Town 8001, South Africa

http://www.cambridge.org

© Cambridge University Press 2001

First published 2001
Reprinted 2001

Printed in the United Kingdom at the University Press, Cambridge

Typeface Delima MT   *System* QuarkXPress®

A catalogue record for this book is available from the British Library

ISBN 0 521 80569 4 paperback

ACKNOWLEDGEMENTS
The publishers gratefully acknowledge the following for permission to reproduce copyright material.

Textual material

Newspaper extracts from 'Blair faces villa sleaze probe' (p.16) by Patrick O'Flynn (*Daily Express* 7 Jan. 2000, p.2); 'Hospital facing beds crisis as flu cases soar' (p.16) by Rachel Ellis (*Daily Express* 7 Jan 2000, p.7); 'New boy Gary scores winner and outshoots Des Lynam' (p.16) by Ben Summerskill (*Daily Express* 7 Jan. 2000, p.23); 'Crimebuster aged just 13, Schoolgirl wages war on crooks' (p.16) by Martin Stote (*Daily Express* 7 Jan. 2000, p.27); 'Hole lotta trouble' (p.16) (*Daily Star* 7 Jan. 2000, p.11); 'Postie's down under blunder' (p.16) (*Daily Star* 7 Jan. 2000, p.23); 'Dome sweet Dome... for the people' (p.16) (*Daily Mirror* 7 Jan. 2000, p.7); 'Kate's Mosstery man' (p.16) (*Daily Mirror* 7 Jan. 2000, p.19); 'Boy lama flees across Himalayas to escape Chinese' (p.16) (*Daily Telegraph* 7 Jan. 2000, p.1) © Telegraph Group Ltd., 7 January 2000, by permission of the Daily Telegraph. 'Beckham sees red once more' (p.16) (*Independent* 7 Jan. 2000, p.1). 'Threat of Ice Titan' (p.20) by James Chapman (*Daily Mail* 24 Mar. 2000, p.37), reproduced by permission of Atlantic Syndication on behalf of the *Daily Mail*. 'Stop him' (p.24) by John Kay (*Sun* 24 Mar. 2000, pp.4, 5). © News International Newspapers Ltd., 24 Mar. 2000, by permission of the *Sun*. 'I'll be your valentine' advertisement (p.26), by permission of the National Canine Defence League; Marwell Zoo brochure (p.28), by permission of Marwell Zoological Park; Fanta advertisement and logo (p.33), by permission of The Coca-Cola Company, 'Fanta' is a registered trademark of The Coca-Cola Company, 'diet Fanta' is a trademark of The Coca-Cola Company; Jacobs Twiglets advertisement (p.33), by permission of Jacobs Bakery Ltd; Clarks shoes advertisement, by permission of Clarks International. Slogans used (p.27): 'Beanz meanz Heinz' by permission of Heinz; 'A Mars a day helps you work, rest and play'® is a registered trademark of Mars UK Ltd, used with permission; 'Go to work on an egg' by permission of the British Egg Information Service; 'Drinka pinta milka day' by permission of the Residuary Milk Marketing Board; 'Have a break. Have a Kit-Kat' by permission of Société des Produits Nestlé S.A.; 'Ronseal. It does exactly what it says on the tin' by permission of Ronseal; 'Persil washes whitest' by permission of Lever Fabergé. *The Hound of the Baskervilles* (pp.52, 53) by John O'Connor (Nelson Thornes), by permission of Nelson Thornes. Extracts from *The Hound of the Baskervilles* (p.55) by Sir Arthur Conan Doyle (Oxford University Press) copyright © 1996 The Sir Arthur Conan Doyle Copyright Holders, by permission of Jonathan Clowes Ltd., London, on behalf of Andrea Plunket, administrator of the Sir Arthur Conan Doyle copyrights.

Photographs

MI5 Chief Stephen Lander (p.24), by permission of The Press Association; Laptop, Paddington station and MI5 headquarters (p.24) by permission of the *Sun*; Eric Cantona sequence 'As bad as it gets'(p.42) by permission of *Match of the Day* magazine, BBC; Faces on Marwell Zoo brochure (p.28), by permission of Pebble Graphics Design Consultants.

Every effort has been made to trace copyright holders, but in some cases this has proved impossible. The publishers would be happy to hear from any copyright holder that has not been acknowledged.

NOTICE TO TEACHERS
The photocopy masters in this publication may be photocopied free of charge for classroom use within the school or institution which purchases the publication. Worksheets and photocopies of them remain in the copyright of Cambridge University Press and such photocopies may not be distributed or used in any way outside the purchasing institution. Written permission is necessary if you wish to store the material electronically.

Contents

	Page
GENERAL NOTES	
Contents of the Student's Book	4
How Literacy in Context fits the National Curriculum	5
The National Literacy Strategy	6
Literacy in Context – contents of the books in the series	7
Your scheme of work – different ways of using the Student's Book	8
Notes on the Student's Book	9–10
Cross-curricular opportunities	11
Writing frames	12

COPYMASTERS 13–60

Four for each of the units in the Student's Book
- Checking the language – for low attainers
- Further language practice
- Homework and revision
- The text*

Plus
- Assessing your own work – four sheets

NEWSPAPERS

1 What's in a newspaper?	13–16
2 Reporting the news	17–20
3 Writing for an audience	21–24
Assessing your own work	25

ADVERTISING

4 Who needs to advertise?	26–29
5 Selling the product	30–33
6 TV advertising and comedy	34–37
Assessing your own work	38

THE MOVING IMAGE

7 Match of the day	39–42
8 Screen horror	43–46
9 Shakespeare in action	47–50
Assessing your own work	51

COMPARING TEXTS

10 Book, theatre, radio and cinema	52–55
11 Ways of selling	56–59
Assessing your own work	60

Glossary 61–63

* The texts have been reproduced from the Student's Book to enable students to take them home and use them alongside any relevant copymasters. They will also be useful as OHTs for class discussion.

Contents of the Student's Book

	Unit	Text types	Word	Sentence	Text	Activities
Newspapers	1 What's in a newspaper? Pages 8–13	Newspaper cuttings & a complete article *All in a day's work*	• Puns • Rhyme	• Sentence subject • Adjectival phrases	• Types of article	Create headlines and opening sentences
	2 Reporting the news Pages 14–19	Newspaper report *Iceberg!*	• Synonyms	• Quotes	• Content & structure • The intro	Write a newspaper report
	3 Writing for an audience Pages 20–25	Newspaper report *Stop thief!*	• Colloquial language	• Register	• Paragraphs	Write an article in informal register
Advertising	4 Who needs to advertise? Pages 26–31	A selection of adverts *Argos, beans and cornflakes: an ABC of advertising*	• Emotive words	• Slogans	• The print media • Advertising sites • Image and copy	Create a magazine advert for a charity or a campaign
	5 Selling the product Pages 32–37	Two magazine adverts *Fanta House and Twiglets Treble*	• Jargon	• Imperative sentences	• Typography • Logos • Graphics	Draft a proposal for a magazine advertisement
			Media skills			
	6 TV advertising and comedy Pages 38–43	Television advertising *How jammy can you get?*	• The moving-image media • Humour in television advertising • Genres • Parody • The spelling of loan words			Write an analysis of a television advertisement
The moving image	7 Match of the day Pages 44–49	A sequence from a televised football match *Kung-fu Cantona*	• Terminology (frame, sequence, shot) • Editing			Plan to televise an incident from history
	8 Screen horror Pages 50–55	Storyboard of the final sequence of a horror film *Frankenstein*	• Shots • Framing • Cutting	• Montage • Genres		Plan a film sequence in a well-known genre
	9 Shakespeare in action Pages 56–61	Storyboard of the opening sequence of a film version of Shakespeare *Macbeth and the witches*	• Shots • Framing • Camera angle	• Interpretation • Location, props and costumes • Casting		Write an analysis of the opening of a film version of *Macbeth*
Comparing texts	10 Book, theatre, radio and cinema Pages 62–73	A novel text A stage dramatisation A radio adaptation A film version *The Hound of the Baskervilles*	• Stage dramatisation (location and physical space, stage directions) • Radio adaptation (sound effects, dialogue) • Film version (montage, framing, shots)			Adapt an extract from *The Hound of the Baskervilles* for radio
	11 Ways of selling Pages 74–79	A magazine advertisement and a television advertisement for the same product *How to get your new shoes noticed*	• Target groups • Message • Images	• Captions • Duration		Write an article comparing the magazine advertisement with the television advertisement

How Literacy in Context fits the National Curriculum

En1 Speaking and Listening

Knowledge, skills and understanding

Speaking

Fluency/appropriacy/context
- structure talk clearly
- use illustrations and anecdotes to enrich ideas
- use gesture, tone and pace
- use visual aids to enhance communication
- use a varied vocabulary
- use standard English in different contexts
- self-evaluate

Listening

Listen/understand/respond
- recall main features, e.g. of text, TV, radio
- explicit and implicit understanding
- recognise persuasion, humour and argument
- distinguish tone, undertone and implications
- recognise vagueness and ambiguity
- ask and answer questions

Group discussion and interaction

Participation
- make different contributions according to listeners and activity
- take different views into account and modify own views
- sift and summarise
- take on different roles in group
- clarify others' ideas

Drama
- use dramatic techniques to explore ideas and issues
- convey action, character, atmosphere and tension
- recognise how structure contributes to dramatic effect
- evaluate drama performances

Standard English
- use in formal and informal situations

Language variation
- use of standard English in public communication
- influences on spoken and written language
- attitudes to language use
- differences between speech and writing
- standard English vs dialectal variation
- the development of English

Breadth of study

Speaking
- describe, narrate, explain, argue, persuade, entertain
- extended talk
- presentations to different audiences

Listening
- listen to and watch live talks and presentations
- recordings, e.g. radio, TV, film
- discussions involving spontaneous responses

Group discussion and interaction
- explore, hypothesise, debate, analyse
- take different roles in groups

Drama activities
- improvisation and working in role
- devise, script and perform in plays
- evaluate own and others' performance

En2 Reading

Knowledge, skills and understanding

Understanding texts

Reading for meaning
- recognise implied and explicit meanings
- analyse and discuss alternative interpretations
- how ideas and values are explored
- how individuals, community and society are presented
- how meanings change when adapted for different media
- read complete novels, plays and poems

Understanding the author's craft
- language use
- issues, motivation and plot
- author's stance
- variation of techniques, structure, forms and styles
- comparing and contrasting texts

Language structure and variation
- knowledge of grammar and language variation develops understanding of texts and how language works

Media and moving image texts
- meaning conveyed in print, image and sound
- form, layout and presentation contribute to effect
- nature and purpose influence content and meaning
- audience response

Breadth of study

Literature
- 2 Shakespeare plays (1 at Key Stage 3)
- drama by major playwrights
- pre-1914 fiction by 2 major writers
- 2 post-1914 works of fiction by major writers
- pre-1914 poetry by 4 major poets
- post-1914 poetry by 4 major poets
- recent and contemporary drama, fiction and poetry for young people and adults
- drama, fiction and poetry by major writers from different cultures and traditions

English literary heritage
- influential texts, e.g. Greek myths, Bible, legends
- texts of high quality and their long-term appeal

Texts from different cultures and traditions
- understand values and assumptions in the texts
- significance of subject matter and language
- distinctive nature
- how themes are explored
- comparing and contrasting

Non-fiction and non-literary texts
- literary non-fiction
- print and ICT-based information and reference texts
- media and moving image texts, e.g. newspapers, advertisements, TV, films

Printed and ICT-based information texts
- select, compare and synthesise information
- evaluate presentation of information
- sift relevant from irrelevant
- identify features at word, sentence and text level

En3 Writing

Knowledge, skills and understanding

Composition

Writing to imagine, explore, entertain
- draw on own experience of fiction, poetry and drama
- use imaginative vocabulary
- choose language and structure to appeal to reader
- use a range of techniques

Writing to inform, explain, describe
- form sentences and paragraphs to express connections
- use formal and impersonal language
- include relevant details
- present material clearly

Writing to persuade, argue, advise
- develop logical arguments and cite evidence
- use persuasive techniques
- anticipate reader reaction

Writing to analyse, review, comment
- reflect on subject matter
- form own view
- distinguish between analysis and comment
- take account of the reader

Planning and drafting
- plan, draft and proofread on paper and screen as necessary
- analyse own and others' writing

Punctuation
- use full range of punctuation

Spelling
- learn and apply knowledge of patterns, word families, roots, affixes and inflections
- spell complex, irregular words
- use dictionary, thesaurus and spell checker

Handwriting and presentation
- write fluently and quickly
- ensure work is neat, legible and well-presented

Standard English
- select appropriate degree of formality

Language structure
- parts of speech and their functions
- structure of phrases and clauses and how to combine them
- paragraph structure
- structure of whole texts
- use appropriate grammatical terminology

Breadth of study

Writing to imagine, explore, entertain
- stories, poems, playscripts, autobiographies, screenplays, diaries

Writing to inform, explain, describe
- memos, minutes, accounts, leaflets, prospectuses, plans, records, summaries

Writing to persuade, argue, advise
- brochures, advertisements, editorials, articles and letters conveying opinions, campaign literature, polemical essays

Writing to analyse, review, comment
- reviews, commentaries, articles, essays, reports

Thinking skills
- use writing for thinking and learning, e.g. paraphrasing, taking notes

Readership
- write for specific readers, an unknown readership and oneself

The National Literacy Strategy

The language features and activities in the opening five units of the Student's Book offer you a structured programme of language work, matched closely to the Word, Sentence and Text level objectives in the National Literacy Strategy Framework for Teaching English.

Parts 1, 2 and 3 of the Student's Book each contain three units, differentiated according to the full range of levels relevant for Key Stage 3.

Part 4 contains two units which focus on comparing texts.

Assessment models are provided at the end of Parts 1, 2, 3 and 4 to support target-setting for students and teachers.

Points to note about the Word, Sentence and Text activities in this book

- It is only the first five units of this book which are structured according to the NLS Word, Sentence and Text principle.
- The remaining units (Units 6 to 11), which are partly or wholly image-based, have a different 'grammar', for which the division into Word, Sentence and Text areas is not a helpful one.
- In these later units, an introduction to basic design concepts enables students to analyse print media advertising, and a grasp of techniques such as framing and montage enables them to describe, analyse and respond to a variety of moving-image texts.

Exceptions

Occasionally, language features in Units 1 to 5 are placed under a heading different from that in the NLS Framework.

- In Unit 3, for example, colloquial language is explored as a Word feature. This is because the focus here is at word level (on vocabulary).
- Also in Unit 3, paragraphing is dealt with as a Text feature (rather than under Sentence, as in the NLS), because the focus is on the paragraph structure of the whole text, rather than the sentence make-up of individual paragraphs.

Literacy in Context
Contents of the books in the series

Language to imagine, explore and entertain
Celeste Flower

ISBN	0 521 80560 0	student's book
	0 521 80561 9	teacher's portfolio

Autobiography *Stories for children*
Science report *TV drama script*
Mind Map® *Ballads*
Discussion *Fiction*

Language to inform, explain and describe
Gary Beahan

ISBN	0 521 80558 9	student's book
	0 521 80559 7	teacher's portfolio

Survey *Newspaper article*
Interview *Eyewitness account*
Instructions *Web site*
Travel guide *Prospectus*

Language to persuade, argue and advise
Shelagh Hubbard

ISBN	0 521 80562 7	student's book
	0 521 80563 5	teacher's portfolio

Advertisement *Leaflets*
Newspaper articles *Advisory texts*
Debate speech *Web site*
Letters *Fiction*

Language to analyse, review and comment
John O'Connor

ISBN	0 521 80554 6	student's book
	0 521 80555 4	teacher's portfolio

Newspaper articles *Reviews*
Reports *Letters*
Campaign leaflet *Commentaries*
Essay *Biography*

Language of media and the moving image
John O'Connor with **Graham Charlton**

ISBN	0 521 80568 6	student's book
	0 521 80569 4	teacher's portfolio

Newspapers and magazines
Print media advertisements
Campaign leaflets
Television advertisements
Television sports report
Films
Web sites
Adaptations for media: stage, radio and film

Language of literary non-fiction
Grainne Nelson with **Ian Aspey**

ISBN	0 521 80566 X	student's book
	0 521 80567 8	teacher's portfolio

Autobiography *Diaries*
Biography *Account*
Newspaper report *Travel*
Journals *Sports journalism*

Language of pre-1914 literature
Pauline Buckley and **Celeste Flower**

ISBN	0 521 80556 2	student's book
	0 521 80557 0	teacher's portfolio

Poetry **Drama**
  Rudyard Kipling   *G B Shaw*
  Thomas Gray   *Victorian melodrama*
  Chaucer   *Shakespeare*
  J Scott and T Sackville

Prose
  Kenneth Grahame
  Gilbert White
  Emily Brontë
  R L Stevenson
  Charles Dickens

Language of Shakespeare
Rex Gibson

ISBN	0 521 80564 3	student's book
	0 521 80565 1	teacher's portfolio

Language and story
  Spells and songs
  Soliloquy
  Storytelling

Language and imagination
  Insults
  Imagery
  Comedy and repetition

Language and structure
  Dramatic openings
  Lists
  Dialogue

Comparing the language
  Shakespeare's verse
  Prose
  Sonnets

Your scheme of work – different ways of using the Student's Book

The units	Wider uses
1 What's in a newspaper?	• link with puns in Unit 5 • link with humour in Unit 6 • short text cuttings - ideal as a Year 7 introduction
2 Reporting the news	• comparison with a televised report in Unit 7 • dramatic 'threatening iceberg' report
3 Writing for an audience	• link with television advertising in Unit 6 • accessible colloquial language
4 Who needs to advertise?	• link with advertising in Unit 11 • link with slogans in Unit 11 • colourful image-based text
5 Selling the product	• link with advertising in Unit 11 • focus on images and graphics • link with football in Unit 7
6 Advertising and comedy	• link with advertising in Unit 11 • humour as a major focus
7 Match of the day	• link with frames and shots in Units 10 and 11 • a television sequence in 16 frames
8 Screen horror heritage	• link with pre-1914 texts from the literary heritage in Unit 9 • link with novels of horror and suspense in Unit 10 • focus on images from *Frankenstein*
9 Shakespeare in action	• link with adaptation from one medium to another in Unit 10 • link with writing an analysis in Unit 11 • a useful new perspective on *Macbeth*
10 Book, theatre, radio and cinema	• links with Units 6, 7, 8 and 9 (see above) • all the work based on *The Hound of the Baskervilles*
11 Ways of selling	• links with Units 4, 5, 6, 7 and 9 (see above) • a comparison of how print media and moving-image media advertise the same product

Notes on the Student's Book

Reasons for choosing the texts

- The newspaper cuttings and full articles have been selected for their accessibility and interest levels.
- The featured advertisements (Fanta, Twiglets, Jammie Dodgers) are for products familiar to Key Stage 3 students.
- The television sequence of Eric Cantona's kung-fu style kick is dramatic and justly famous.
- The *Macbeth* storyboard offers a different approach to the study of this popular Shakespeare play at Key Stage 3, while *Frankenstein* links with the study of pre-1914 texts.
- *The Hound of the Baskervilles* is an enduringly popular mystery story and the ideal base from which students can learn about the natures of the different performance media of theatre, radio and screen.
- The two advertisements for Clarks shoes have been selected because, while designed for different media, they come from the same advertising campaign.

Background information on some of the units

Unit 1

The newspaper cuttings were all taken from the same day's publications and represent the full range of tabloids and broadsheets.

On copymaster 1.1, the adjectival phrases quoted are described as adjectival because they give us more information about the noun. In other sentences they could be noun phrases, for example **The former England captain** now presents Match of the Day.

Unit 2

It will be possible to get an updated report on the giant iceberg from web sites such as the *National Geographic* web site.

Units 4, 5, 6 and 11

The special group vocabulary featured in Unit 5 is known as a **sociolect**. Some students might benefit from knowing the term, but it is by no means essential. The concept itself is important to grasp, however, as it is closely tied in with the notion of target groups. The **age target groups** that advertisers use are: up to 15; 16–24; 25–35; 36–55; over 55.

It is straightforward to explain the notion of target groups established according to **gender**.

Class is the third major group, and some students might find it helpful to know about the conventionally accepted social class categories:

    A   lawyers, doctors, accountants
    B   teachers, nurses, police officers
    C1   clerical workers (clerks, typists)
    C2   plumbers, car mechanics, carpenters
    D   lorry drivers, postal workers
    E   casual workers and unemployed people

It is harder for a Year 9 student to categorise advertisements according to class target groups, but certain ones (such as fashion ads in teen magazines) are clearly aimed at people on limited incomes.

All target grouping involves **stereotyping**. It has not been dealt with in the Student's Book, but teachers might well want to question whether advertisers are right to assume there are characteristics to certain ages, genders and classes, predictable enough that whole advertising campaigns can be founded upon them.

Unit 8

There are two widely available *Frankenstein* films. Kenneth Branagh's film for Columbia TriStar Films (UK) is based upon Mary Shelley's novel, which first appeared in 1818. The first ever *Frankenstein* film appeared in 1910, but the one which really established the genre was the 1931 version, starring Boris Karloff and directed by James Whale.

Unit 9

Roman Polanski's *Macbeth* (Columbia Pictures, 1971) has a 15 certificate, because of some nudity and a rape scene. In 2001 Channel 4 televised the RSC production, with Antony Sher and Harriet Walter.

Unit 10

Sir Arthur Conan Doyle's famous story *The Hound of the Baskervilles* first appeared in 1902. It is published in Penguin and Oxford World Classics editions.

Unit 11

It will be interesting to compare the 'New Shoes' campaign with later ones by Clarks or other shoe manufacturers, focusing in particular on the major selling-points.

Background reading

- An excellent introduction to moving-image texts is *Film Art: an Introduction*, by David Bordwell and Kristin Thompson (McGraw-Hill, 1990), currently in its 4th edition.
- Cary Bazelgette has examined the relationship between moving-image study and English in a thought-provoking article in *English in Education* (Vol. 34, No. 1, 2000), called 'A Stitch in Time: Skills for the New Literacy'.

Cross-curricular opportunities

Unit 1 What's in a newspaper?
Subject link – PSHE
- Hold a class discussion on crime and whether a person as young as 13 should be organising a Neighbourhood Watch group.

Unit 2 Reporting the news
Subject links – geography, science
- Trace the position of the iceberg on a map of the world and work out the directions in which it might be heading.
- Look up *icebergs* on a CD-ROM encyclopedia. How are they formed? Why are they so dangerous?

Unit 3 Writing for an audience
Subject links – ICT, history
- Find out about encryption of email. What is it and who uses it?
- Do some research to find out more about MI5. What do they do?

Unit 4 Who needs to advertise?
Subject links – PSHE, art, graphics
- Hold a class debate with the motion that 'Advertising is a total waste of money'.

Unit 5 Selling the product
Subject links – PSHE, art, graphics
- Design a magazine advertisement for a new product, paying particular attention to the image and the graphics.

Unit 6 TV advertising and comedy
Subject link – PSHE
- Hold a class discussion on whether there are more products which ought to be banned from advertising on television (as cigarettes are at present).

Unit 7 Match of the day
Subject links – PE and games, history, RE
- Discuss which events from history, or episodes recounted in different scriptures, would have made good television. What would we have been able to see? How differently would the people involved have behaved if they had known they were being filmed?

Unit 8 Screen horror
Subject links – history, English literature, art
- Watch a complete film. Do some research to find out more about Mary Shelley. How did *Frankenstein* come to be written?
- Watch parts of Kenneth Branagh's version and the 1931 film version directed by James Whale. What differences do you notice in the way Frankenstein himself and the monster are portrayed?

Unit 9 Shakespeare in action
Subject links – history, English literature, art
- Watch the complete film of *Macbeth*. What part do the witches play in his downfall? Do they simply foretell what is going to happen, or do they actually help to persuade Macbeth to be a killer?
- Find out about the historical Macbeth. Do the history books say that he was a good king or a bad one?

Unit 10 Book, theatre, radio and cinema
Subject link – English literature
- Read Sir Arthur Conan Doyle's *The Hound of the Baskervilles*, or some of the Sherlock Holmes short stories, such as *The Speckled Band*.
- Hold a class discussion about other sightings of mysterious animals that you have heard about. Do you know of any local legends about such creatures?

Unit 11 Ways of selling
Subject link – PSHE
- Hold a class discussion on whether you are ever influenced by advertising. Give examples of advertisements which have been effective in encouraging you to buy the product, and others which have turned you off.

Writing frames

Writing frames form a key part of this series. Their value in providing structure and cohesion to students' writing is well established, and the National Literacy Strategy Framework promotes their use. Appropriately used, writing frames possess great power to improve students' writing. Keeping the following guidance in mind will help you ensure that the writing frames you use will help your students' writing skills.

Writing frames work best when:

- their structure gives students a clear sense of the final product
- the sentence starters allow students to develop their own thoughts and ideas
- they are used for drafting rather than for the finished product
- students first read and analyse the features of the text with which the frames are used
- they are part of a wide and varied diet of writing activities

Alternative uses of some of the frames

- Frames such as the one for Unit 3 can easily be adapted, for example by asking students to complete the opening two or three paragraphs, rather than the whole thing.

For low attainers

- The frame for Unit 1 is not for a complete text, but for sentence structures. The Unit 2 frame is for a short article. These are therefore useful where full-length pieces of writing might not be appropriate.
- In some cases (Units 6 and 11, for example), sentence-starters are suggested. These can be adapted to suit individual student needs.
- The Unit 10 frame offers a few suggested opening lines.

Further ideas for some of the frames

- Some of the frames (Units 5 and 8) focus on text layout as well as content.
- Others (Units 5, 7 and 8, for example) require a graphic response in addition to the verbal one.
- Frames for graphics-based work (such as the one for Unit 5) offer a framework without sentence-starters, as the linguistic element is less significant.

Checking the language

1.1

> An **adjectival phrase** is a group of words which tells us more about the noun.

For example, we might write:

> *Johnson* (noun), *captain for the first time in her career* (adjectival phrase), *was determined to take the Cup*.

An adjectival phrase will often be added to the subject of a sentence to provide additional information, like this:

Subject	Adjectival phrase	Rest of the main clause
Spencer Smith,	the former world triathlon champion,	has retired from competition.

Sometimes in newspaper articles the adjectival phrase comes first:

Adjectival phrase	Subject	Rest of the main clause
Suspected Nazi war criminal	Konrad Kalejs	fled Britain yesterday.

1 Add an adjectival phrase to each of the following unfinished sentences. Try to make the resulting sentence as funny or as unlikely as possible. The first one has been completed to give you an idea.

Subject	Adjectival phrase	Rest of the main clause
Robbie Williams,	the well-known singer,	has become Prime Minister at the age of 42.
David Beckham,		
The Queen,		
The England football team,		

2 These sentences have already been started off with an adjectival phrase. Complete them by adding a subject and the rest of the main clause.

Adjectival phrase	Subject	Rest of the main clause
White-haired grandmother		
Ageing rock-star		
Blond, blue-eyed		
Champion marbles player		

Further language practice   1.2

> Because headlines take up a lot of space, journalists often use a kind of **shorthand**.

This involves choosing short, punchy words instead of longer ones. Many of these shorthand words are not often found in day-to-day speech or other kinds of writing. For example, the headline *Brits to woo teeny fan bands* means that the people who organise the Brit Awards (*Brits*) are planning to attract (*woo*) bands with young (*teeny*) fans.

Study the shorthand words in these headlines and write down what each one is short for. The first one has been done to start you off.

Noun	Headline	Meaning of the word
Fergie	**Fergie** clashes with Express football editor	Football manager, Alex Ferguson
probe	Blair faces villa sleaze **probe**	
ban	Pressure group hails **ban** on GM farmers by Tesco	
fury	**Fury** as Nazi war crimes suspect slips from Britain	
row	Tyson faces KO in UK entry ban **row**	
quest	**Quest** for missing woman	
scare	New beef **scare**	
bid	Brown in **bid** to win the title	

Verb	Headline	Meaning of the word
clashes	Fergie **clashes** with Express football editor	
soar	Hospital facing beds crisis as flu cases **soar**	
flees	Boy lama **flees** across Himalayas to escape Chinese	
slips	Fury as Nazi war crimes suspect **slips** from Britain	
hails	Pressure group **hails** ban on GM farmers by Tesco	
wed	Hollywood star to **wed** Welsh lass	
sees red	Beckham **sees red**	
axed	Rail service to be **axed**	
vows	PM **vows** to cut taxes	
curb	Police to **curb** drink-driving	

Homework and revision

1.3

> Newspapers are made up of many different kinds of article.
> A **report** is an account of something that has happened, such as a football match, a demonstration or a hurricane. A **features** article is not about news. It can cover anything that the readers might be interested in, from fashion to the weekly horoscope.

1 If you were to open a newspaper today, you would probably find examples of all the articles listed below. Invent a headline to go with each one. For example, a political news report about the Prime Minister's planned visit abroad might have the headline *PM to visit Israel*, while a sports feature on an athlete's bid to win an Olympic medal might be headed *Digging for gold*.

A day's articles

- A political news report
- A sports news report
- A health news report
- The lead story – on the front page; chosen as the most important or dramatic story that day
- International news – a report on something that has happened overseas
- Media news – of interest to readers, most of whom will be keen television-watchers
- A sports feature
- Industrial news – about transport or industry
- The 'Leader' article – in which the newspaper expresses its opinions on subjects of the day
- A human interest story – something about ordinary people
- A 'celebrity' story – about somebody from the world of sport or entertainment
- Arts news – about music, cinema or the theatre
- A light-hearted story

2 Find an example of each of these articles in one of this week's newspapers. Then write down the headline that goes with each one.

Spelling

W is not the only letter which can be silent. Write down three other examples for each of the following silent letters.

Silent letter	Examples	Your examples
g	gnash, design	
k	knock	
l	walk, calf, yolk	
b	lamb	

© Cambridge University Press 2001

Headlines and articles

1.4

Hospital facing beds crisis as flu cases soar
Daily Express, p7

Boy lama flees across Himalayas to escape Chinese
Daily Telegraph, p1

Hole lotta trouble
Daily Star, p11

Dome sweet Dome... for the people
Daily Mirror, p7

New boy Gary scores winner and outshoots Des Lynam
Daily Express, p23

POSTIE'S DOWN UNDER BLUNDER
Daily Star, p23

Kate's Mosstery man
Daily Mirror, p19

Top of the pups
Daily Mirror, p11

BECKHAM SEES RED ONCE MORE
Independent, p1

Crimebuster aged just 13
Schoolgirl wages war on crooks

BY MARTIN STOTE

A schoolgirl has stolen a march on criminals by becoming Britain's youngest Neighbourhood Watch co-ordinator.

Emily Webster, 13, decided to act when she was left depressed and troubled by several raids on her home.

She sought help from a victim support group to overcome her fear, and then visited the crime prevention officer at her local police station.

She designed an anti-crime pamphlet, delivered leaflets to residents, and has now been adopted as the co-ordinator for her area.

Emily, who attends Woodrush School in Hollywood, Birmingham, joined the war on crime after one burglary and two attempted break-ins at her home. She is now organising a meeting to launch the Neighbourhood Watch operation and to determine how big a patch to cover.

Her mother Jo said: "The break-in had a terrible effect on Emily. But the help from the victim support group was great and turned her round. She became determined to beat these evil people."

Ian Garrett, manager of Victim Support for South Birmingham said: "Emily was depressed, frightened and withdrawn because of what happened. Now she is confident and outgoing."

Daily Express, p27

Checking the language

2.1

> Journalists often use a **combination of language and illustrations** to get the main points of their report across to the reader.

The writer James Chapman does this to explain where the iceberg is and how enormous it is.

Looking at the language

The left-hand column of this grid lists six things writer James Chapman does to help us understand the iceberg's great size.

- Match each one up with one of the quotations from the article printed on the right.
- Draw arrows linking each writing feature with its quotation.

Writing feature *To get across the idea of the iceberg's great size, he:*	Quotation from the report
• compares the iceberg with the size of a country that we know	• The huge slab of ice covers more than 4,000 square miles
• tells us its area	• 'This is a very big iceberg, close to a record, if not a new record. It's not often that you see them of this magnitude.'
• tells us the iceberg's exact length and breadth	
• tells us the iceberg's thickness	• it will dwarf the 40-mile-long iceberg which broke away in October
• compares it with last year's iceberg	• An iceberg half the size of Wales
• quotes a scientist who is himself talking about world records	• at 183 miles long and 22 miles wide will be one of the largest bergs on record in the Southern seas
	• the 900-feet thick chunk

Looking at the illustrations

On your photocopy of the article, the maps and photograph are labelled A, B, C and D. Tick boxes in this grid to show which pictures help us to understand:

	A	B	C	D
• where the iceberg is				
• which direction it is heading in				
• how big it is				
• what it looks like, seen next to the ice-shelf				

© Cambridge University Press 2001

Further language practice 2.2

> Journalists often use a method of structuring their reports known as **pyramid writing**.

It is called this because, of the 100 per cent of readers who read an article's headline, only 70 per cent might read to the end of the intro, and only 50 per cent will carry on to the end of the third and fourth paragraphs. This situation can be represented in an upside-down pyramid:

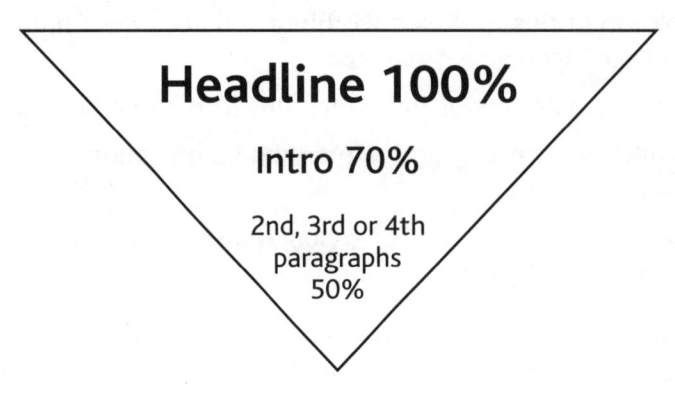

Headline 100%

Intro 70%

2nd, 3rd or 4th paragraphs 50%

This means that the most dramatic facts are in the headline and intro, the next most dramatic facts are in paragraphs two and three and so on.

1 Complete the following diagram to see how James Chapman has used pyramid writing in his report:

100% read the headline, which uses the following dramatic language:
e.g. ....

70% might read the intro, which contains these dramatic facts:
e.g. ....
....

50% might read paragraphs 2, 3 and 4, which add these details to the main facts:
e.g. ....
....
....

2 Write a plan in note form for a newspaper report of a giant asteroid which scientists say might be on course to collide with the Earth. Think about the rules of pyramid writing when you decide on the content of each paragraph. Finally draft the article, remembering the other features of report writing that you learned about in the unit.

Homework and revision 2.3

> When you write an article, you can either **quote** a person's exact words or use **reported speech**.

Notice the different ways in which quotes and reported speech are written down.

- **Quotes** are written and punctuated in the same way as dialogue in fiction.
- **Reported speech** is different. You do not need speech marks because you are not quoting the speaker's exact words.

For example, the first scientist might have said: *I am worried about icebergs this size.* See what happens when this is turned into reported speech:

The original quote	What you do to change it into reported speech	The final reported speech version
He said:	• introduce it with *X said*:	He said
	• (sometimes) add *that*	that
'I	• remove the speech mark and change the pronoun from first person (*I*, *we*) to third person (*he*, *she*, *they*)	he
am worried about	• shift the verb back a tense to change it from present to past	was worried about
icebergs this size.'	• (sometimes) change the phrasing and remove the closing speech mark	such gigantic icebergs.

1 Turn the following quotations into reported speech:
 - Matthew Lazzara said: 'I think this is a record.'
 - 'It can travel fifteen miles a day,' he added.
 - Dr Vaughan said: 'This has not happened in a hundred years.'

2 Write a brief (100–150 word) speech on any subject of your choice. Then imagine that it was reported in the local newspaper. Write the journalist's report. To make your writing interesting and varied, use a mixture of quotes (your exact words, correctly punctuated) and reported speech.

Spelling

Design a poster to go on your classroom wall which helps people to learn the spellings of words which contain the *gh* or *ght* combination.

For example, you could draw cartoons with speech bubbles and captions underneath, full of *gh* and *ght* words.

Daily Mail, Friday, March 24, 2000 — Page 37

Threat of ice titan

Berg half the size of Wales may go adrift

By James Chapman

AN ICEBERG half the size of Wales is threatening to break away from Antarctica and start drifting towards some of the world's busiest shipping lanes, scientists warned last night.

The huge slab of ice covers more than 4,000 square miles and at 183 miles long and 22 miles wide will be one of the largest bergs on record in the Southern seas.

Scientists were alerted by satellite pictures which revealed massive fissures around the 900-feet thick chunk.

They believe it is only a matter of time before the block of ice breaks free to become the largest of a string to have separated from the Antarctic ice shelf in recent years.

Once adrift, it will dwarf the 40-mile-long iceberg which broke away in October but melted before hitting any ships.

Scientists are increasingly worried about climate changes across Antarctica where temperatures have risen by 2.5 degrees Centigrade over the past 50 years. Many believe that global warming is melting the glacier which has seen five ice shelves collapse since 1930.

Matthew Lazzara of the University of Wisconsin's Antarctic Meteorological Research Centre which analysed the satellite data, said: 'This is a very big iceberg, close to a record, if not a new record. It's not often that you see them of this magnitude.'

He said, once free from the Ross ice shelf, it could travel up to 15 miles a day. It will either head north towards Brazil, or be dragged by deep ocean currents towards South Africa.

The danger would come if it entered warmer seas where it would be broken up into smaller pieces that would pose a far greater hazard to shipping.

Drifting icebergs can also cause major changes in weather patterns as they move into warmer climates. Temperatures drop by up to five degrees Centigrade and fog forms around the ice.

Dr David Vaughan of the British Antarctic Society in Cambridge, said: 'There's no doubt that this is the birth of a very large iceberg. It is interesting because the Ross ice shelf rarely produces them. It is probably around 100 years since one broke away.'

However, Dr Vaughan said he was unconvinced that global warming was responsible.

'The big question is how often these icebergs are breaking off,' he said. 'If something of this magnitude was happening every year, then I would start to be worried, but at the moment it is not.'

BREAKING LOOSE . . . THE MONSTER ICEBERG

A — [map showing CHILE, ARGENTINA, Falklands, Tierra del Fuego, Drake Passage]

B — South Pole, Ross Ice Shelf; Iceberg could drift with current towards the tip of South America

C — Satellite image of ice sheet 183 miles long, 22 miles wide and 900ft deep which is breaking away from the Ross Ice Shelf

D — To scale: The giant ice sheet is half the size of Wales

Checking the language

3.1

> A **simple sentence** consists of one clause: it says just one thing and contains only one main verb. When we join two or more simple sentences together with *or*, *and* or *but*, we get a **compound** (or co-ordinated) **sentence**. When we use a different **conjunction** (a joining word, such as *because* or *when*) to show how two or more clauses are joined together, we make a **complex sentence**.

Here are some examples of different types of sentence from the article about the stolen computer:

- *The theft is extremely regrettable.*
This is a simple sentence, because it has only one clause (one main verb: *is*).

- *In a flash he had snatched the bag from beside the agent's feet and hared away.*
This is a compound sentence, because it has two clauses, joined by *and*.

- *As he fumbled in his pockets for change, the sharp-eyed opportunist criminal spotted his chance.*
This is a complex sentence, because it has two clauses, joined by the conjunction *as*.

All of the following sentences appeared in *The Sun* newspaper on the same day. In pairs, decide whether they are simple, compound or complex sentences and give your reasons. The first one has been completed to start you off.

Sentence	Simple, compound or complex	Reason
Lee got the tiny wound while he was fighting with his brother, Mark.	*complex*	*It has two clauses, joined by the conjunction* while
A deadly, flesh-eating piranha fish has spurned meat and now munches only cucumbers and tomatoes.		
Your gamecard has a printed line of six lottery numbers, unique to you.		
Sinead O'Connor has a new fella – and it's yet another journalist.		
Tot Adele Humphries was saved by her nappy when she plunged 15 feet from a window onto a concrete path.		
Supermum Mel Gannon has collected an astonishing 13,000 Free Books for Schools tokens.		

© Cambridge University Press 2001

Unit 3 Writing for an audience
Language of media and the moving image

Further language practice (3.2)

> A very common type of complex sentence used by journalists is one which includes a main clause and an **adverbial clause of time** (introduced by a conjunction such as *when*, *as*, *since* or *while*).

A good example is one of the complex sentences in the article on page 20, which starts off with the adverbial clause *As he fumbled in his pockets for change,...*

1 Underline the adverbial clauses of time in the following sentences, all taken from *The Sun* newspaper on the same day:

- Coronation Street star Tracy Shaw set tongues wagging when she was seen with a wedding ring.
- Bo Walsh, 19, will fill in on the lads' tour supporting Oasis in America while Neil Primrose becomes a dad.
- Pam and Charles Ward got their Morris Traveller back yesterday when workers found it in a Glasgow canal.

2 Make up some opening sentences for newspaper reports which have the following headlines. Each one should be a complex sentence which includes an adverbial clause. (Remember that adverbial clauses can be introduced by conjunctions such as *when*, *as*, *since* or *while*.)

There is a suggestion for the first one, to give you an idea:

ALIENS LANDED IN MY FRONT GARDEN!
As he left his house for work yesterday, Bernard Tomkins bumped straight into an alien spacecraft.

ELVIS SIGHTED IN BLACKPOOL AMUSEMENT PARK

WOMAN ATTACKED BY KILLER BEES

WORKMEN COMPLAIN OF GHOST NUISANCE

GERBILS TO THE RESCUE!

Spelling

Write down these other words to do with computers, check their meanings and learn their spellings:

- site (*compared with* sight)
- cursor
- modem
- icon
- monitor
- scroll
- software
- virus

Homework and revision

3.3

Tabloids and broadsheets: some facts

- The terms **tabloid** and **broadsheet** refer to the newspaper's size and format. If you take the front page of *The Guardian* (a broadsheet), fold it in half and turn it on its side, you get a tabloid page.

- **Broadsheet newspapers** include daily national newspapers such as: *The Times*, *The Financial Times*, *The Guardian* and *The Daily Telegraph*, and national Sunday newspapers such as *The Sunday Times*, *The Observer* and *The Independent on Sunday*.

- **Tabloid newspapers** include national dailies such as *The Mirror*, *The Sun*, *The Star*, *The Mail* and *The Express*, and national Sunday newspapers such as *The News of the World*, *The People* and *The Sunday Mirror*.

- The difference between broadsheets and tabloids is not simply one of size and format. They are also aimed at different audiences. Broadsheets are mainly targeted at social groupings A, B and C1. Tabloids are mainly for groups C2, D and E.

  To give you a rough idea what these terms mean, group A includes doctors and accountants; C1 includes secretaries and people in skilled jobs; C2 includes plumbers; and E consists of unemployed people and casual workers.

- *The Express* and *The Daily Mail* are sometimes termed 'middle-of-the-road' tabloids because they are aimed at people who might otherwise read a broadsheet newspaper.

See for yourself what the differences are between broadsheet and tabloid newspapers. Here are some of their characteristics. Get hold of copies of a broadsheet and a tabloid, and find examples of each of these features.

Broadsheets tend to have:	Tabloids tend to have:
• a higher proportion of longer articles • more in-depth coverage • whole sections about overseas news, business, the arts and finance	• shorter articles • very short paragraphs • a higher proportion of light-hearted 'human interest' stories • a more obvious focus on scandal and sex stories • a much bolder layout, with bigger headlines

An informal news report

The text 3.4

THE SUN, Friday, March 24, 2000

ANOTHER SUN EXCLUSIVE

STOP HIM

MI5 agent's desperate cry as thief grabs laptop with state's top secrets

Station chase... thief struck as spy was buying ticket at busy Paddington

By JOHN KAY
Chief Reporter

A FRANTIC spy yelled "Stop Thief!" as he chased a crook who had pinched his MI5 computer across a busy station.

The red-faced intelligence agent bawled desperately to cops to help him as he dashed after the agile robber.

Two bobbies on duty at London's Paddington Station scrambled to join in the crazy race through crowds of amazed tube travellers. But the thief – who had grabbed a £2,000 laptop crammed with Government secrets – nimbly dodged and twisted as his three pursuers tried to converge on him.

In seconds, with commuters and families staring open-mouthed and stumbling out of his way, he sprinted into a warren of walkways and vanished. The Keystone Cops2 style caper came after the MI5 "spook" had put down the laptop – full of dossiers on Northern Ireland and other sensitive issues – as he bought a ticket. As he fumbled in his pocket for change, the sharp-eyed opportunist criminal spotted his chance. In a flash he had snatched the bag from beside the agent's feet and hared away.

Last night a massive hunt was under way to recover the computer as MI5 squirmed with embarrassment over the latest astonishing security blunder.

A squad of over 150

Report... MI5 chief Stephen Lander

Embarrassed... the service's HQ

Special Branch and police officers was trying to locate the computer which was being carried by a middle-ranking operative of MI5, the Government's home intelligence service.

Officials insisted the material stored on the laptop was so well encrypted, or coded, that nobody could access or make use of it.

But other experts claimed the code COULD be cracked and feared the secrets would no longer be safe.

And a senior security source admitted: "The theft is extremely regrettable. We want the laptop back."

MI5 director general Stephen Lander has given a full report on the incident to Home Secretary Jack Straw. And Mr Straw in turn has briefed PM Tony Blair, overall head of security services.

THIEF'S PRIZE
Opportunist crook swiped £2,000 laptop computer like this from spy

RAF MAN'S GOOF

The theft is the most embarrassing security breach since a laptop was nicked from RAF man David Farquhar ten years ago.

The Wing Commander lost his job after the computer containing secrets of the Allies' Gulf War plans was swiped from his official car.

Farquhar had stopped his Vauxhall to visit a car showroom in Acton, West London. A thief smashed windows and pinched the laptop and two briefcases.

Unit 3 Writing for an audience
Language of media and the moving image

Assessing your own work

Newspapers

When teachers and examiners mark and assess your work, they sometimes give it a level. Look carefully at this chart and decide at which level you would place yourself. First judge your work against the criteria in the **Word** column, then **Sentence** and finally **Text**.

- Your teacher might also use this chart.
- The language skills that you have been practising are highlighted in **bold**.
- In the box marked **Targets**, make a note of the language skills which you need to revise, or the new skills that you now want to develop.

Learning about the language of newspapers

	WORD	✓	SENTENCE	✓	TEXT	✓
Level 3 Reading					You can understand the main points in a text.	
Level 3 Writing	You choose a variety of interesting words. You spell most common words correctly.		Most of your sentences are correctly put together, following the rules of grammar. You use capital letters, full stops and question marks correctly to show the beginnings and ends of sentences.		Your writing is well organised and clear. It shows that you have thought about who is going to read it.	
Level 4 Reading					You can pick out the most important ideas in a text. You refer back to the text when explaining your views. You know what a **feature article** in a newspaper is.	
Level 4 Writing	You use words for particular effects (including **puns**). You spell all common words correctly.		You use punctuation within sentences (full stops, capital letters and question marks). You can write sentences which contain a **subject**, **verb** and **adjectival phrase**.		Your writing is lively and thoughtful. You develop your ideas in interesting ways.	
Level 5 Reading			You know the difference between **quotes** and **reported speech** in a newspaper report. You understand the **structure** of a news article.		You can select sentences and information to support your views. You can retrieve and collect together information from a range of different sources.	
Level 5 Writing	You choose imaginative **vocabulary** and use words precisely (including **synonyms**). You usually spell complex, regular words correctly.		You use a range of punctuation correctly (including apostrophes and inverted commas). You use simple and complex sentences confidently.		You can judge when to use a formal style. You organise sentences into **paragraphs**. You can judge when to use the first person or the third person. You take into account who is going to read your writing.	
Level 6 Reading	You can pick out **colloquialisms**.				You can summarise a range of information from different sources.	
Level 6 Writing	You vary your **vocabulary** to create particular effects. You usually spell complex irregular words correctly.		You use punctuation such as semi-colons to make your meaning clear. You use a range of sentence structures – **simple**, **compound** and **complex** – to achieve different effects.		Your writing captures the reader's interest and keeps it. You use an impersonal style where appropriate. You organise your ideas into **paragraphs**.	
Level 7 Reading					You can understand the ways in which meaning and information are conveyed in a range of texts. You can select and put together a range of information from a variety of sources.	
Level 7 Writing	Your spelling is nearly always correct. You choose **vocabulary** with great care and accuracy.		You select sentence structures to suit the ideas you want to convey and the **style** of writing.		You judge when to use particular forms and **different registers**. You use **paragraphs** to make the development of your ideas clear to the reader.	

Targets

Checking the language

4.1

> Advertisers and other writers use **emotive words** when they want to have a particular effect on our feelings and emotions.

For example, the advertisement for holidays in Egypt contains a large number of words which make us feel that Egypt is a place of warmth and beauty.

Here is an extract from an advertisement for a cruise through the Norwegian fjords, which is packed with adjectives which conjure up a picture of the amazing sights.

> *This superb seven-night cruise allows you the luxury of relaxing on your own floating hotel as some of Europe's most dramatic scenery comes to you. Majestic mountains, ancient glaciers, sparkling fjords and cascading waterfalls will all be enjoyed on this cruise and there will be plenty of time to explore.*

1. Find the emotive adjectives to describe:
   - the seven-night cruise
   - the scenery
   - mountains
   - glaciers
   - fjords
   - waterfalls

2. Make up a different set of emotive words which could be used if you wanted to put people off the holiday cruise and write them into the spaces. For example, you could describe the scenery as boring, rather than dramatic.

> *This .... seven-night cruise allows you the luxury of relaxing on your own floating hotel as some of Europe's most .... scenery comes to you. .... mountains, ... glaciers, ... fjords and .... waterfalls will all be enjoyed on this cruise and there will be plenty of time to explore.*

Further language practice 4.2

> Advertising **slogans** are short, catchy phrases which are designed to stick in the memory.

Softees shoes use the slogan *the Soft option*; and one of the most famous of all advertising slogans was the extremely simple: *Guinness is good for you*.

Here are some slogans from television advertisements. Write down what you think it was that made them so catchy and memorable. For example, was it the sounds of the words put together? Was there something unusual about the phrase? Was there a humorous 'story' to go with the slogan? Or was the slogan effective because it was very simple?

Beanz meanz Heinz.

A Mars a day helps you work, rest and play.

Go to work on an egg.

Drinka pinta milka day.

Have a break. Have a Kit-Kat.

Ronseal. It does exactly what it says on the tin.

Persil washes whitest.

Spelling

Add your own examples to the following table, which shows the different ways in which to form plurals. Write in four examples for each type of word.

Type of word	How you form the plural	Examples	Your examples
most common words	add -s	book, cat, sea	
words ending in -ss	add -es	boss	
words ending in -x		box	
words ending in -ch		church	
words ending in -sh		dish	
words ending in -y	drop the -y and add -ies	lady	

© Cambridge University Press 2001

Homework and revision

4.3

1 Write notes around this advertisement for Marwell Zoo, giving your comments on:
- the slogan
- emotive words
- the image
- the copy
- the strap-line (a final line to wrap everything up and underline an important feature)

The slogan at the top of the right-hand page works because it makes us think about...	The image is very simple...

The copy has information on...

Marwell brings you extra fun and activity during your visit to the Park. Our events calendar highlights these special occasions.
Please tick the appropriate box on the tear-off slip to tell us which events you would like to know more about and send it to:

Special Events 2000
Marwell Zoological Park
Colden Common, Winchester,
Hampshire, SO21 1JH

or you can e-mail us with your postal address and a note of the events for which you require details at:

events@marwell.org.uk

Emotive words such as *fun*...

In addition to our Special Events we also run

CREATURE CLOSE-UPS
Informal introduction to Marwell and "hands on" session for adults and children - tickets can be bought at the gate. School holidays and at weekends from February to October.

TOUCH TABLES*
FACE PAINTING*
FREE ROAD TRAIN
RAIL TRAIN*

*VARIABLE SEASONAL ACTIVITY

The strap-line at the base of the left-hand page...

MARWELL
ZOOLOGICAL PARK

Colden Common, Winchester, Hampshire, SO21 1JH.
Telephone: 01962 777407

A FULL DAY OUT WITH SOMETHING FOR EVERYONE

ARE YOU PREPARED?
SPECIAL EVENTS 2000
MARWELL ZOOLOGICAL PARK

2 Make a collection of print media advertisements which appeal to you and, for each one, make a note of the feature you admire most. It might be the clever language, the image, or the combination of the image and the copy. Then compare your opinions with other people's. What kinds of things do people like and dislike about advertisements?

Advertisements

The text 4.4

I'll be your Valentine

Will you be mine?

Sponsor a dog like me today – and you'll gain a truly loving friend…

That's right, for just £1 a week you can sponsor an abandoned dog like me. You'll be helping the NCDL to give an abandoned dog who may never be rehomed a safe and happy life at one of their 15 Rehoming Centres. You'll also help thousands of other dogs who are cared for by the NCDL every year. In return, you'll get a sponsor's certificate, updates on your dog – and a very faithful friend. So if you want true love for ever, sponsor a dog today.

YES, I'd L♥VE a best friend

☐ Please send me my FREE poster guide so I can choose a dog to sponsor today.

Mr/Mrs/Miss/Ms/Other _____

Address _____

_____

_____ Postcode _____

Please return this form to: Sponsor A Dog, NCDL, FREEPOST LON6996, London E1 8BR. www.ncdl.org.uk

Registered Charity No. 227523   887900

NCDL — National Canine Defence League — A Dog is for Life

SPONSOR A DOG

© Cambridge University Press 2001

Unit 4 Who needs to advertise?
Language of media and the moving image

Checking the language

5.1

> A **pun** is the use of two words with different meanings but similar sounds to get a humorous effect.

Advertisers sometimes use puns to amuse us and capture our attention. A good example is the wordplay on the two meanings of 'the Treble' in the advertisement for Twiglets.

1 To help you understand how puns work in advertising, fill in the following chart of puns found in advertising slogans for Thornton's chocolate eggs and for Twiglets. Write down the usual meaning of the slogan and an example that you might hear in everyday speech. Then explain its punning meaning in the advertisement.

To give you the idea, an example has been filled in from the advertisement for K Softees shoes.

The advertisement	The slogan	Its usual meaning	An example of its usual meaning	Its punning meaning in the advertisement
K shoes	The soft option	The easy way out	Instead of complaining, he took the soft option and walked out of the shop.	You will be choosing comfortable shoes made of soft fabrics.
Thornton's eggs	Get cracking!			
Twiglets	In the bag Give 'em some stick			

2 Can you think of any other magazine or television advertisements which use puns in this way? Add as many as you can to the following chart.

The advertisement	The slogan	Its usual meaning	An example of its usual meaning	Its punning meaning in the advertisement

Further language practice 5.2

> Advertisements often contain **imperative** sentences: ones which tell you or ask you to do something.

1 Find the imperatives in the Fanta advertisement. (There aren't any in the body copy.) Write down the ones which are used:

- as the biggest and most striking part of the copy, to encourage you to take part
- to give you instructions about what to do

2 Find the imperative used on the Twiglets bags. Write down what that phrase usually means. Where would you be most likely to hear it used?

3 Make a list of imperatives from other advertisements you have seen. Write a sentence or two to explain why you think advertisers use imperatives so often.

Spelling

Homophones are words which sound the same but have different spellings and meanings.

1 Write down the spellings of the words which complete the homophone pairs in the chart below. Then compose a sentence which uses both words. For example, for *beech* and *beach*, you might write *The beech tree was growing by the beach.*

Homophone pair		Sentence
beech	beach	The beech tree was growing by the beach.
shoot		
horse		
muscle		
alter		
seen		
allowed		

2 Make up some puns using homophones.

For example: *Did you hear about the bald man who painted rabbits on his head because from a distance they looked like hares?*

Homework and revision 5.3

> When we want to talk about the special kinds of lettering used in advertising and the print media, we use the term **typography** (the study of the way words are typed, drawn or printed).

For example, on page 27 of your book the type in the Yorkie Bar advertisement is designed to look like the lettering on the bar itself, and the clock times on the HP Baked Beans advertisement (*7.15 p.m.* etc.) look as though they come from a badly printed timetable or schedule.

1. People who design advertisements think very carefully about typography. Here are seven reasons for choosing particular kinds of type. Try to find an example of each one in the advertisements for Fanta and Twiglets. The first one has been completed to start you off:

The advertisement	Word or phrase in particular type	The reason for choosing that style of type
Twiglets	*Twiglets (on the bag itself)*	The lettering looks twig-like.
		The slogan looks like newspaper headlines.
		The traditional lettering reflects the old established company name.
		The wavy lettering suits the exciting flavours.
Fanta		The short, punchy imperative sentences look lively and remind you of partying.
		The particular words and phrases which might appeal to the young reader are picked out in larger, bolder type.
		Important information is printed very clearly.

2. How many other examples of cleverly chosen typography can you add to the chart below? Look first at the examples on the advertisements printed on pages 32–33 of the Student's Book. Then study the type on the covers of books in the classroom. Finally add details about the type on cereal and soap powder packets.

The advertisement	Word or phrase in particular type	The reason for choosing that style of type

Advertising in magazines

The text

5.4

Unit 5 Selling the product
Language of media and the moving image

Checking the language

6.1

> Different kinds of narrative are called **genres**.

Possible genres include:

- science fiction
- fantasy
- war story
- detective story
- disaster movie
- horror
- action movie
- romance
- historical story
- police movie
- western
- epic
- spy thriller
- supernatural story
- hospital drama

Which genre would have the following typical features? Write down the name of the genre and then the title of a film or television programme in that genre.

The first one has been done to start you off.

Typical features	Genre	Example
aliens, distant planets, force fields	science fiction	*Star Wars*
magic, rings of power, dwarfs		
classical heroes, the gods		
plane crashes, volcanoes, sinking ships		
secrets, codes, people in disguise		
criminals, investigators, clues		
a setting in the distant past		
monsters, mad scientists		
horses, canyons, wagon trains		
ghosts, poltergeists, inexplicable happenings		
soldiers, planes, battles		
two people who overcome obstacles and fall in love		
car chases, shoot-outs, explosions		

Further language practice 6.2

> Each genre has its own recognisable and typical features. A comedy film or book which mocks the typical features of a particular genre is called a **parody**.

The titles of films can sometimes tell you which genre is being parodied. For example, the reference to the famous 15th-century navigator in the title *Carry on Columbus* tells us that it is a parody of historical films.

Think carefully about the clues in the following film titles and write down which genre you think they might be parodying.

- Blazing Saddles
- Life of Brian
- Beverly Hills Cop
- Young Frankenstein
- Space Balls
- Naked Gun
- Carry on Doctor
- Airplane

Possible genres include:

- science fiction
- fantasy
- war story
- detective story
- disaster movie
- horror
- action movie
- romance
- historical story
- police movie
- western
- epic
- spy thriller
- supernatural story
- hospital drama

Spelling

Here are some more foreign words and phrases which are often used in English. Use a dictionary to find the meaning of each one and the language it comes from. Then learn the spellings.

Word	Meaning	Language it comes from
eureka!		
faux pas		
Homo sapiens		
per annum		
sang-froid		
status quo		
terra firma		

Homework and revision 6.3

> Many television advertisements use **humour** to amuse the audience and interest them in the product.

Write a short letter to the *Radio Times* entitled *Why I like (or don't like) humour in television advertising*.

Starting points
First ask yourself the following questions:

- How funny is the Jammie Dodgers Dips advertisement, in your opinion?
- How does it compare with other television advertisements which use humour?
- What different kinds of humour do we find in advertisements? Think about examples of verbal humour and visual humour.
- What is your favourite humorous television advertisement?
- Do humorous advertisements work, in your experience? In other words, do they encourage you to buy the product?

Clues for success
Think about advertisements which:

- parody a well-known genre, such as the one for Jammie Dodgers Dips
- build up a whole series, based on a catch-phrase (such as *I bet he drinks Carling Black Label*) or a single idea (such as Weetabix giving you the strength to do anything you want).

Don't forget the correct layout for formal letters. Here is a typical layout:

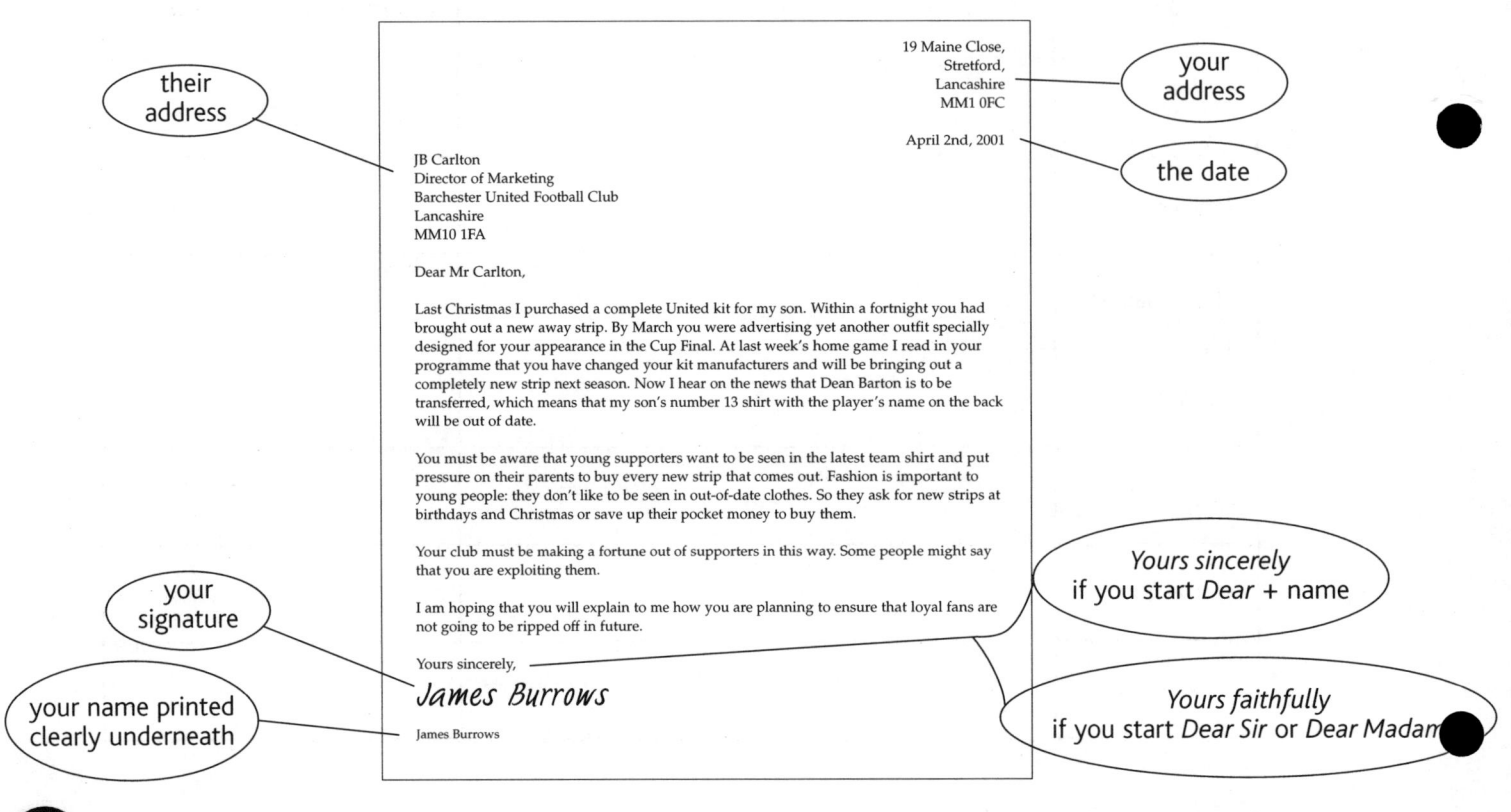

(their address)

(your address)
19 Maine Close,
Stretford,
Lancashire
MM1 0FC

(the date)
April 2nd, 2001

JB Carlton
Director of Marketing
Barchester United Football Club
Lancashire
MM10 1FA

Dear Mr Carlton,

Last Christmas I purchased a complete United kit for my son. Within a fortnight you had brought out a new away strip. By March you were advertising yet another outfit specially designed for your appearance in the Cup Final. At last week's home game I read in your programme that you have changed your kit manufacturers and will be bringing out a completely new strip next season. Now I hear on the news that Dean Barton is to be transferred, which means that my son's number 13 shirt with the player's name on the back will be out of date.

You must be aware that young supporters want to be seen in the latest team shirt and put pressure on their parents to buy every new strip that comes out. Fashion is important to young people: they don't like to be seen in out-of-date clothes. So they ask for new strips at birthdays and Christmas or save up their pocket money to buy them.

Your club must be making a fortune out of supporters in this way. Some people might say that you are exploiting them.

I am hoping that you will explain to me how you are planning to ensure that loyal fans are not going to be ripped off in future.

Yours sincerely,

James Burrows (your signature)

James Burrows (your name printed clearly underneath)

Yours sincerely if you start *Dear* + name

Yours faithfully if you start *Dear Sir* or *Dear Madam*

Making an advertisement for television

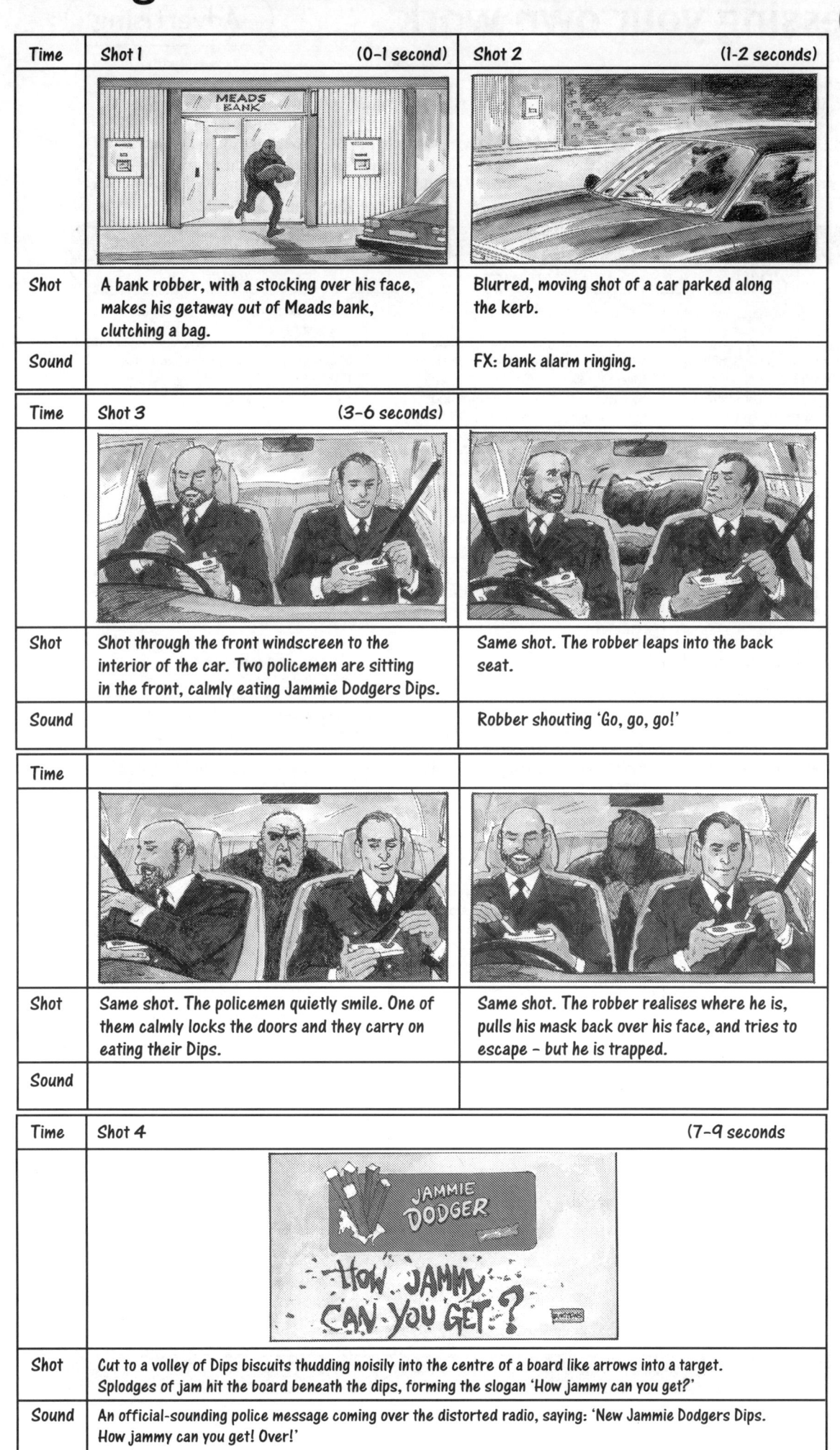

6.4

Time	Shot 1 (0–1 second)	Shot 2 (1–2 seconds)
Shot	A bank robber, with a stocking over his face, makes his getaway out of Meads bank, clutching a bag.	Blurred, moving shot of a car parked along the kerb.
Sound		FX: bank alarm ringing.

Time	Shot 3 (3–6 seconds)	
Shot	Shot through the front windscreen to the interior of the car. Two policemen are sitting in the front, calmly eating Jammie Dodgers Dips.	Same shot. The robber leaps into the back seat.
Sound		Robber shouting 'Go, go, go!'

Time		
Shot	Same shot. The policemen quietly smile. One of them calmly locks the doors and they carry on eating their Dips.	Same shot. The robber realises where he is, pulls his mask back over his face, and tries to escape – but he is trapped.
Sound		

Time	Shot 4 (7–9 seconds)
Shot	Cut to a volley of Dips biscuits thudding noisily into the centre of a board like arrows into a target. Splodges of jam hit the board beneath the dips, forming the slogan 'How jammy can you get?'
Sound	An official-sounding police message coming over the distorted radio, saying: 'New Jammie Dodgers Dips. How jammy can you get! Over!'

Assessing your own work

Advertising

When teachers and examiners mark and assess your work, they sometimes give it a level. Look carefully at this chart and decide at which level you would place yourself. First judge your work against the criteria in the **Word** column, then **Sentence** and finally **Text**.

- Your teacher might also use this chart.
- The language skills that you have been practising are highlighted in **bold**.
- In the box marked **Targets**, make a note of the language skills which you need to revise, or the new skills that you now want to develop.

Learning about the language of advertising

	WORD	✓	SENTENCE	✓	TEXT	✓
Level 3 Reading					You can understand the main points in a text.	
Level 3 Writing	You choose a variety of interesting words. You spell most common words correctly.		Most of your sentences are correctly put together, following the rules of grammar. You use capital letters, full stops and question marks correctly to show the beginnings and ends of sentences.		Your writing is well organised and clear. It shows that you have thought about who is going to read it.	
Level 4 Reading					You can pick out the most important ideas in a text. You refer back to the text when explaining your views. You can find and use ideas and information.	
Level 4 Writing	You use words for particular effects. You spell all common words correctly.		You use punctuation within sentences (full stops, capital letters and question marks). You are beginning to use complex sentences.		Your writing is lively and thoughtful. You develop your ideas in interesting ways.	
Level 5 Reading	You understand the use of **emotive words** and **jargon**.				You can select sentences and information to support your views. You understand how **choice of form**, **layout** and **presentation** contribute to effect.	
Level 5 Writing	You choose imaginative **vocabulary** and use words precisely. You usually spell complex, regular words correctly.		You use a range of punctuation correctly (including apostrophes and inverted commas). You use simple and complex sentences confidently.		You can judge when to use a formal style. You organise sentences into **paragraphs**. You can judge when to use the first person or the third person. You take into account who is going to read your writing.	
Level 6 Reading			You understand the use of **imperative sentences**. You can identify different styles of **typography** and understand their uses. You understand the use of features such as **font**, **caption** and **illustration** in printed texts.		You can summarise a range of information from different sources. You can understand the combined use of **text** and **images**. You can identify the major **genres**.	
Level 6 Writing	You vary your **vocabulary** to create particular effects. You usually spell complex irregular words correctly.		You use punctuation to make your meaning clear. You use a range of sentence structures to achieve different effects.		Your writing captures the reader's interest and keeps it. You judge when to write in different forms. You use an impersonal style where appropriate. You organise your ideas into **paragraphs**.	
Level 7 Reading					You can understand the ways in which meaning and information are conveyed in a range of texts. You can select and put together a range of information from a variety of sources.	
Level 7 Writing	Your spelling is nearly always correct. You choose **vocabulary** with great care and accuracy.		You select sentence structures to suit the ideas you want to convey.		You judge when to use particular forms and different styles of writing. You use **paragraphs** to make the development of your ideas clear and coherent to the reader.	

Targets

Checking the language

7.1

Use this framework to show how you would televise a moment from history.

In the large panel:
- Draw a sketch-plan of the scene.
- Show where your four cameras are placed and write brief notes to explain their positions.

In the section at the bottom:
- Draw sketches to show what each of the first six shots looks like.
- Add the number of the camera taking the shot and how many seconds of the sequence have passed.
- Write a brief description of what the camera sees, to go with your drawing.

Sketch-map of the scene
Cameras
1   2
3   4

The first six frames					
00 secs	.... secs	.... secs	.... secs	.... secs	.... secs
Camera	Camera	Camera	Camera	Camera	Camera ....
Description					

Unit 7 Match of the day
Language of media and the moving image

Further language practice 7.2

> A series of frames which tells part of a story is called a **sequence**.

A sequence is like a scene in a play or an episode in a novel. It tells one part of the whole story and is linked to what comes before it and after it.

> A single uninterrupted run of the camera is called a **shot**.

At any one moment in a televised sporting event, there will be several cameras, all taking different shots.

> Each individual picture can be called a **frame**.

It is really only films which have frames: each individual one can be seen if you hold out a strip of film. A television works quite differently. Even so, the term *frame* can still be used to describe each single split-second picture on television.

Think about something which has been in the news recently. It might be a sporting event or a disaster somewhere in the world, such as a flood or hurricane. Make some notes to describe what a short news report might look like on television. Don't try to describe it in detail. Simply give a short account of the sequence and then make brief notes under the two headings of *Shots* and *Frames*.

- Shots: write something about the different camera shots.
- Frames: make a note of some of the most interesting and striking frames.

Look back at the Eric Cantona sequence to remind yourself about shots and frames. Here is an example of what you could do, based upon the report of a flood.

Sequence	A short sequence showing the extent of the flood and the way it is affecting individual people		
Shots	1 From a plane flying over the flooded land	2 From a dinghy going through the flood waters to rescue people	3 From inside one of the houses
Frames	1 Aerial view of the main street of a village	2 Looking over the prow of the dinghy as it ploughs through the flood waters	3 A householder attempting to rescue some possessions

Now make your own notes in a frame like this.

Sentence

A group of words which makes sense. Sentences can be structured in three ways: they can be **simple sentences**, **compound sentences** and **complex sentences**. A simple sentence is one which contains only one clause, e.g. *The theft is extremely regrettable*. A compound sentence contains two or more main clauses, joined by 'or', 'and' or 'but'. For example, *In a flash he had snatched the case and hared away*. A complex sentence contains a main clause and a subordinate clause, e.g. *As he fumbled in his pockets, the criminal spotted his chance*.

Sequence

A series of frames which tells part of a story, such as a whole scene (Unit 7, p. 46).

Shot

A single uninterrupted run of the camera. You can have **close-ups**, for example, where the camera is very near to the subject, or **long-shots**, taken from further away (Unit 7, p. 47; Unit 8, p. 52; Unit 9, p. 58; Unit 10, p. 69).

Slogan

A short, catchy phrase designed to stick in the memory, e.g. *It's the real thing* (Unit 4, p. 29).

Stage directions

Information given to people performing the play to help them to understand how it can be acted (Unit 10, p. 68).

Subject

The subject of the sentence is 'who' or 'what' the sentence is about, e.g. ***A schoolgirl*** *has stolen the march on criminals...* (Unit 1, p. 10).

Synonym

A word or phrase which means the same, or almost the same, as another word, e.g. *big* and *large* (Unit 2, p. 16).

Target group

The particular audience at which an advertisement is aimed, e.g. *women, 16–24; men over 55* (Unit 11, p. 76).

Typography

The way words are typed, drawn or printed (Unit 5, p. 35).

Verb

The word in the sentence which enables us to say what people or things are doing or being. e.g. *They **think** it's all over...* (Unit 1, p. 10).

Homework and revision 7.3

To help you understand more about moving-image texts, do some research based upon your own television watching.

1. Video a main news programme from any of the television channels. As you watch, make notes on each of the following:

   - **Sequences.** Ignore the times when the camera is on the newsreader – just concentrate on listing the sequences of film used to illustrate the news items. Note how long each sequence is.

   - **Frames.** Make a note of the more interesting frames. Are they ones which give an overall view of the event, for example, or ones which allow us to see people's reactions?

   - **Shots.** Which of the sequences use only one shot (interviews, for example) and which use several different ones?

   - **Editing.** What decisions have been made about how long the various shots should be?

   You could use frames like this to record your notes on each sequence.

Sequence	
Shots	
Frames	
Editing	
General comments	

2. After you have finished your research, write a sentence or two on the most successful sequence in your opinion. For example:

   - Which sequence had the most effective frames and shots?

   - Which sequence was most successful in helping the viewer to understand what was going on?

Capturing a moment on television

7.4

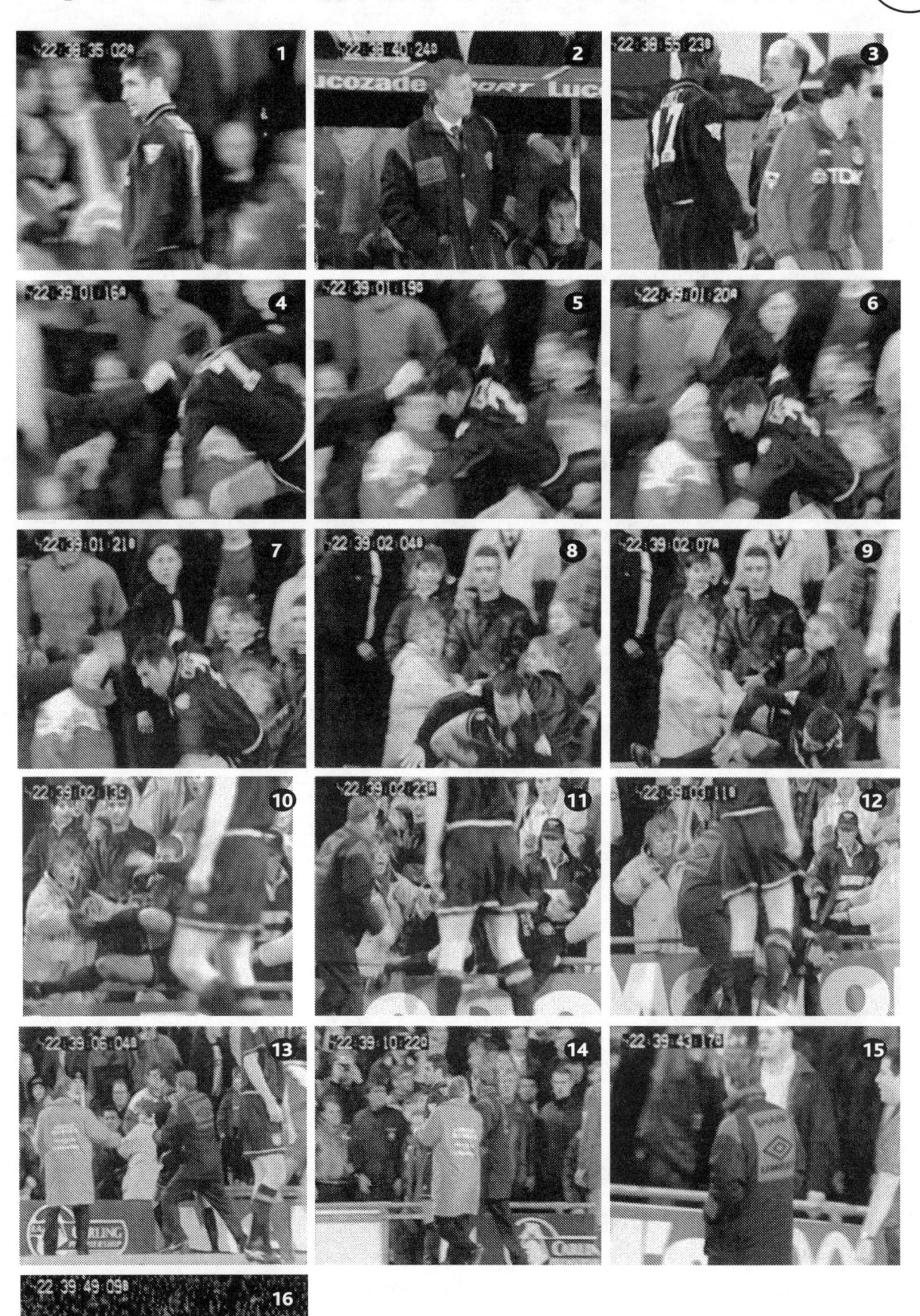

Checking the language

8.1

Use this frame to plan your film sequence. Remember that:

- A variety of **shots** is used to focus on different things. Close-ups show things in detail; distant-shots give a wide view of a scene.
- **Framing** helps the director to gain particular effects. A face might fill the frame to show a person's emotions, or be placed to one side so that other things can be seen at the same time.
- **Montage** is the skill of cutting from one scene to another. It is one of the most important tools the film-maker has for telling a story and creating particular effects.
- **Sound** can include music and dialogue as well as sound effects such as gunshots and howling wind.

Timing				
Image				
Typical feature of the genre				
Shot				
Framing				
Montage				
Sound				

Further language practice 8.2

> Changing from one shot to another is called **cutting**.

For example, the director cuts from a shot of the monster about to jump (frame 11) to a shot of the Captain, showing his reaction (frame 12).

1 Find the frame in which the director holds a shot for the longest time (without cutting to another shot). Write down why you think he stays with this shot as long as he does.

> The skill of joining shots together to get a particular effect is called **montage** (a French word, pronounced *mont-arge*).

Montage can be used to show that time has passed. For example, the director can show someone waiting anxiously on a street corner, and then keep cutting away to a shot of a clock, with its hands in different positions.

2 The final seven shots of the Frankenstein film take only 31 seconds. Write down how you think the montage and the framing help to give the impression that a longer time has passed. Look at:

   - the shots of the departing ship (frames 19, 21 and 23)
   - the shots of the ice-floe (frames 18, 20, 22 and 24)
   - the montage, or cutting from one shot to another

> When a film-maker films a sequence, they will always have a particular **purpose** in mind.

For example, the main purpose of many of the sequences in horror movies might be to frighten or horrify us. Other purposes might include: to entertain us, to make us laugh, to keep us in suspense, to teach us something (about a period in history, for example), or to make us think.

3 With another student, make a list of all the purposes you can think of which you might have in mind if you were a film-maker shooting a particular sequence. Start with the purposes listed above and then add more of your own. Next to each one, write down an example of a sequence in a film that you have seen which seems to fit that purpose. For example:

Purpose	Sequence
To make us laugh	the sequence in *Chicken Run* where…

Homework and revision

8.3

Planning your film sequence

- Think up a new story, but include some typical features of the genre that you have chosen.
- Your 30-second sequence can come from anywhere in the film.
- Use storyboard frames.
- Don't include too much dialogue: in the dramatic *Frankenstein* sequence only one word is spoken.

Remember some of the skills of filming

- Use a variety of shots to help tell the story clearly. Think about the different uses of close-ups and distant-shots, for example.
- Framing helps you to focus the audience's attention. In some shots, you might want a face or an object to fill the frame.
- Think about montage. The way you cut shots together has a powerful effect. For example, you might keep on cutting from a dramatic incident to an onlooker's face and back again.

After you have planned the 30-second film sequence, write an account to explain what you have done.

Starting points

First introduce the film: say what genre it comes from and briefly explain how your sequence fits into the story as a whole. Then write about the main purpose you had in mind (to make people laugh, to frighten them, to keep up the suspense…).

Clues for success

Finally, explain how you used the following to achieve that purpose:

- typical features of the genre
- different shots
- framing
- montage
- sound, music and dialogue

Studying a film

8.4

Time	1 hr 56 mins 35 secs	1.56.38	Time	1.56.44	1.56.48
	①	②		③	④
Shot	Medium-shot: monster standing over the coffin	Full-shot: the monster walks around the coffin	Shot	Distant-shot from at sea: an ice-floe with the ship in the background	Close-up: Walton watches the monster
Sound	Music throughout the sequence		Sound		

1.56.50	1.56.56	1.56.58	1.57.00	1.57.01
⑤	⑥	⑦	⑧	⑨
Medium-shot: the monster gently caresses the coffin	Close-up: the monster's face, full of sadness	Close-up: Walton looks down, himself saddened by the sight	Extreme close-up: The monster looks up and sees Walton for the first time	Close-up: Walton's face, wondering what the monster is about to do
Music throughout the sequence				

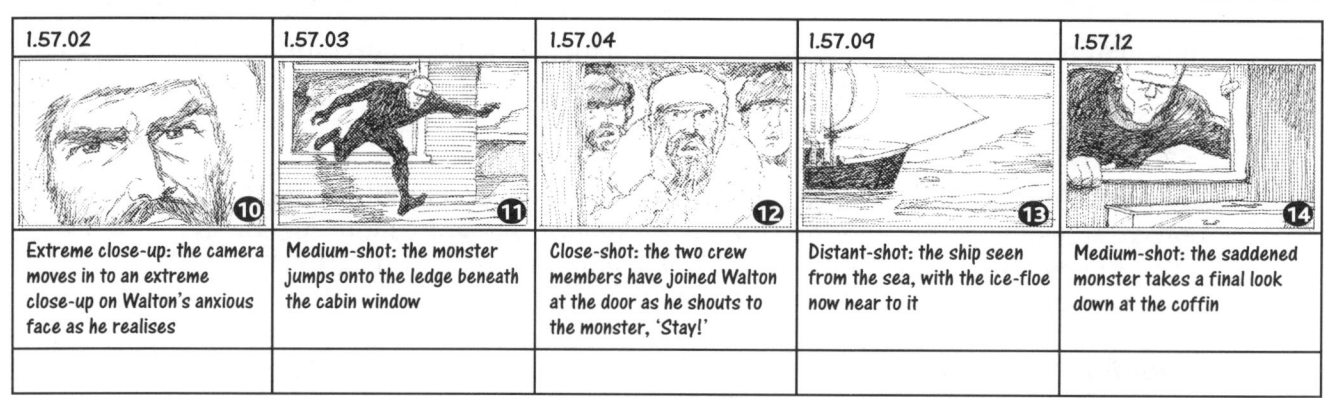

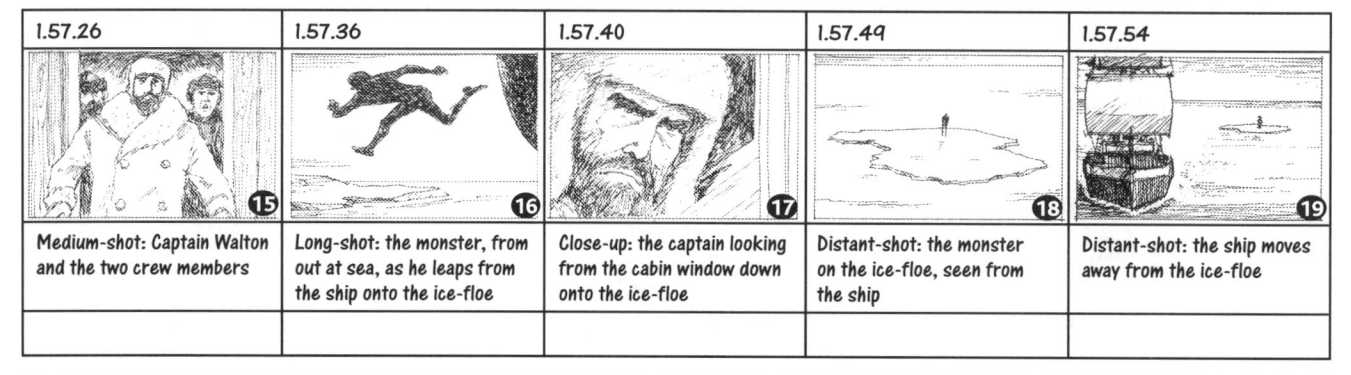

1.57.02	1.57.03	1.57.04	1.57.09	1.57.12
⑩	⑪	⑫	⑬	⑭
Extreme close-up: the camera moves in to an extreme close-up on Walton's anxious face as he realises	Medium-shot: the monster jumps onto the ledge beneath the cabin window	Close-shot: the two crew members have joined Walton at the door as he shouts to the monster, 'Stay!'	Distant-shot: the ship seen from the sea, with the ice-floe now near to it	Medium-shot: the saddened monster takes a final look down at the coffin

1.57.26	1.57.36	1.57.40	1.57.49	1.57.54
⑮	⑯	⑰	⑱	⑲
Medium-shot: Captain Walton and the two crew members	Long-shot: the monster, from out at sea, as he leaps from the ship onto the ice-floe	Close-up: the captain looking from the cabin window down onto the ice-floe	Distant-shot: the monster on the ice-floe, seen from the ship	Distant-shot: the ship moves away from the ice-floe

1.57.58	1.58.01	1.58.04	1.58.10	1.58.13–1.58.20
⑳	㉑	㉒	㉓	㉔
Distant-shot: the ice-floe seen from the ship, now further away	Distant-shot: stern view of the ship sailing away	Same shot as 20, but with the ice-floe now further away	Distant-shot: the ship further away, with the horizon visible behind it	Same shot as 20, the ice-floe now in the distance; the screen fades to black

Checking the language

9.1

> When film-makers are planning a new film, they have to make important decisions about **casting**, **location**, **props** and costumes.

- **Casting** is the name given to the decisions about the people who will act in the film.
- The **location** is the place in which the scene is filmed. This could be anywhere from a busy city street to a tropical island.
- The word **props** is short for *properties* – it means all the objects used in a play, from cups and saucers to swords and shields.
- The **costumes** tell us a great deal about the story and the characters. Are they rich or poor, for example? Are they modern 21st-century people, or do they come from the distant past or a different culture?

Think of three stories that you know really well. They might be novels that you have read or plays and short stories that you are studying at school. (If you get stuck, invent stories of your own.) Make sure that the three stories are very different.

Then imagine that film companies are planning to make films based on each of these stories. Fill in the following tables to show what the companies' early ideas might look like.

Title of the film	
Casting ideas Who do they want in the main part?	
Location Where will the film be shot?	
Props Are there any props that will be particularly important or specially made?	
Costumes Will they be ordinary clothes or something different?	

© Cambridge University Press 2001

Further language practice 9.2

> An **interpretation** of a play is somebody's idea about what it means. We say that a director or an actor is **interpreting** a script by performing it in certain ways and making the audience notice particular things or respond in particular ways.

Whichever interpretation of *Macbeth* directors prefer, they will usually be agreed on three things:

- the story is very frightening
- it raises questions about the supernatural
- it involves terrible violence

Write notes in the following grid to show how the opening of the *Macbeth* film gets all three elements across. For example, if there is something about the camera angles which makes the story frightening, jot it down in the top box of the first column. Two of the boxes have been filled in to start you off. Don't try to write something in every box. Just jot down points where they seem to fit.

Filming *Macbeth*: getting interpretations across to the audience		The story is frightening	It raises questions about the supernatural	It involves terrible violence
Visual effects	Camera angles			Shot 9: the camera shows blood dripping from the head
	Cutting			
	Montage			
	Framing			
	Shots (long/ close-up, etc.)			
	Lighting			
Sound	Music			
	Sound effects		Shot 1: the sound of rooks	
Location				
Props				
Costumes				
Casting				

© Cambridge University Press 2001

Unit 9 Shakespeare in action
Language of media and the moving image

Homework and revision

9.3

Here is the opening of Shakespeare's *Macbeth*.

FIRST WITCH	When shall we three meet again?
	In thunder, lightning, or in rain?
SECOND WITCH	When the hurly-burly's done,
	When the battle's lost and won.
THIRD WITCH	That will be ere the set of sun.
FIRST WITCH	Where the place?
SECOND WITCH	Upon the heath.
THIRD WITCH	There to meet with Macbeth.
FIRST WITCH	I come, Graymalkin.
SECOND WITCH	Paddock calls.
THIRD WITCH	Anon.
ALL	Fair is foul and foul is fair.
	Hover through the fog and filthy air.

[Exeunt]

Create your own opening of a film version of the play which will tell the audience that the story they are about to see:

- is very frightening
- raises questions about the supernatural
- involves terrible violence

Use the grid to make notes on how you might use the different techniques that you have learned about. Include:

- visual techniques such as camera angles, cutting, montage, framing, different shots and lighting
- sound, including music, dialogue and sound effects

Also make notes on what choices you would make to do with:

- location, props, costumes and casting

Draw the opening frames of the sequence in a storyboard like this.

Time	00.00	00......	00......	00......
Frame	1	2	3	4
Shot				
Sound or dialogue				

Shakespeare – script to screen

9.4

Time	00.00	00.15	00.35	00.40
Shot	Dusk. A distant castle silhouetted on a craggy moorland landscape. Rooks wheel around above.	A wooden wedge being hammered into the ground to help support a sturdy, roughly hewn pole.	As the camera holds the shot, looking down at the base of the pole, three pairs of raggedly clothed feet enter the frame.	The camera pans upwards to reveal an old woman (W1) and two younger ones (W2 and W3), staring upwards.
Sound or dialogue	Distant eerie sounds of the rooks and a faint rhythmic hammering sound.	The hammering sound, but louder.	The hammering stops.	

Time	00.45	01.05	01.13	01.30
Shot	The camera moves up the pole to take in a crudely drawn notice, held in place by a nail: 'The traitor Macdonwald'.	Cut to a close-up of a severed head, fixed to the top of the pole.	Cut back to the three women, still staring at the head.	The old woman watches one of the younger ones take a jar out of her sack.
Sound or dialogue				

Time	01.30	01.40	01.45	01.50
Shot	The camera pulls down to show the blood staining the sand, as it drips from the severed head.	The three women's heads framed.	One of the younger women (W2), to the left of the frame.	A shot of all three turning back to look at the head on the pole.
Sound or dialogue	All three: *Fair is foul and foul is fair...*	*...Hover through the fog and filthy air.*	W2: *When shall we three meet again? In thunder, lightning, or in rain?*	W1: *When the hurly-burly's done, when the battle's lost, and won.* W2: *That will be ere the set of sun.*

Time	02.00	02.10	02.50	02.55
Shot	The first two women silhouetted, with the pole between them.	They all trudge off in the direction of the castle.	As they recede, they go out of focus, leaving the head in focus.	The title appears over the image of the head.
Sound or dialogue	W1: *Where the place?* W2: *Upon the heath.* W3: *There to meet with Macbeth.*	Eerie sounds of rooks start up again and continue.		

Assessing your own work — The moving image

When teachers and examiners mark and assess your work, they sometimes give it a level. Look carefully at this chart and decide at which level you would place yourself. First judge your work against the criteria in the **Word** column, then **Sentence** and finally **Text**.

- Your teacher might also use this chart.
- The language skills that you have been practising are highlighted in **bold**.
- In the box marked **Targets**, make a note of the language skills which you need to revise, or the new skills that you now want to develop.

Learning about the language of the moving image

	WORD	✓	SENTENCE	✓	TEXT	✓
Level 3 Reading					You can understand the main points in a text.	
Level 3 Writing	You choose a variety of interesting words. You spell most common words correctly.		Most of your sentences are correctly put together, following the rules of grammar. You use capital letters, full stops and question marks correctly to show the beginnings and ends of sentences.		Your writing is well organised and clear. It shows that you have thought about who is going to read it.	
Level 4 Reading					You can pick out the most important ideas in a text. You refer back to the text when explaining your views. You can find and use ideas and information.	
Level 4 Writing	You use words for particular effects. You spell all common words correctly.		You use punctuation within sentences (full stops, capital letters and question marks). You are beginning to use complex sentences.		Your writing is lively and thoughtful. You develop your ideas in interesting ways.	
Level 5 Reading					You can select sentences and information to support your views. You can retrieve and collect together information from a range of different sources.	
Level 5 Writing	You choose imaginative vocabulary and use words precisely. You usually spell complex, regular words correctly.		You use a range of punctuation correctly (including apostrophes and inverted commas). You use simple and complex sentences confidently.		You can judge when to use a formal style. You organise sentences into paragraphs. You can judge when to use the first person or the third person. You take into account who is going to read your writing.	
Level 6 Reading			You understand features such as **sequencing**, **framing** and **soundtrack** in moving-image texts.		You understand **how meaning is conveyed in texts that include images and sounds**.	
Level 6 Writing	You vary your vocabulary to create particular effects. You usually spell complex, irregular words correctly.		You use punctuation such as semi-colons to make your meaning clear. You use a range of sentence structures to achieve different effects.		Your writing captures the reader's interest and holds it. You are able to **write in different forms** (such as **playscript** and **screenplay**).	
Level 7 Reading					You understand **how audiences and readers respond to different media**.	
Level 7 Writing	Your spelling is nearly always correct. You choose vocabulary with great care and accuracy.		You select sentence structures to suit the ideas you want to convey.		You judge when to use **particular forms** and different styles of writing. You use paragraphs to make the development of your ideas clear and coherent to the reader.	

Targets

Checking the language

10.1

The Hound of the Baskervilles as a stage play

This is a version of the episode in the Student's Book, adapted for performing on stage.

Act 2, Scene 16

Baskerville Hall. A downstairs clock strikes two, there is an unmistakable sound of a creaking stair, and Barrymore enters furtively through a door up L, carrying a candle. He walks across the stage to down R and then kneels, looking out at the audience, as though through a window, pressing his face to the pane.

There is a long silence, as Barrymore peers outwards.

Then, as he lifts the light to the window, Sir Henry enters from the same door, and moves silently up C, followed by Watson.

Sir Henry *(sharply)*   What are you doing here, Barrymore?

Startled, Barrymore swings round to face Sir Henry.

Play scripts use theatre **jargon** to describe parts of the stage, such as *up left* (up L) and *down right*.

To understand this jargon, it helps to remember two things. (1) Many stages used to be sloped up towards the back, so that the audience could see the actors more clearly. (2) The different parts of the stage (left and right) are described from the actors' point of view, not the audience's. So:

- *Up* means the back of the stage. *Down* means the front.
- *Left* and *right* are the actors' left and right – not the audience's.

Copy the following diagram and then use arrows to mark in the movements of Barrymore, Sir Henry and Watson as they are described in the stage directions.

AUDIENCE

	DOWNSTAGE	
LEFT	CENTRE	RIGHT
	UPSTAGE	

Further language practice (10.2)

The Hound of the Baskervilles as a radio play

Here is another episode from earlier in the novel. Turn it into a script for radio.

Sir Henry has left Holmes's apartment with a friend, Doctor Mortimer. Holmes and Watson are shadowing them through the busy London streets, in the hope of spotting the mysterious man who has been following Sir Henry.

Holmes quickened his pace until we had decreased the distance which divided us by about half. Then, still keeping a hundred yards behind, we followed into Oxford Street and so down Regent Street. Once our friends stopped and stared into a shop window, upon which Holmes did the same. An instant afterwards he gave a little cry of satisfaction, and, following the direction of his eager eyes, I saw that a hansom cab with a man inside which had halted on the other side of the street was now walking slowly onwards again.

  'There's our man, Watson! Come along! We'll have a good look at him if we can do no more.'

Remember that you have to use dialogue and sound effects in order to let the listener know what is going on.

This extract from a radio script will remind you how to set it out.
Remember that *FX* stands for sound effects.

[*FX: clock strikes two.*]

SIR HENRY (*despondently*)   No luck, Watson. We'll just have to –

WATSON   Listen!

[*Silence. Then –*
FX: creaking floorboards.]

SIR HENRY (*whispering*)   It's him!

[*FX: slow, soft footsteps and occasional creaks.*]

Homework and revision

10.3

Your favourite novel as a film

Pick a section from a novel that you have enjoyed reading and write an adaptation of it for a film.

- Remember the variety of techniques film-makers use: *camera angles, cutting, montage, framing, varying shots, lighting, timing, sound, music, the location, props, costumes* and *casting*.

- Don't feel that you have to include every line of the novel's dialogue or every idea in the narrative – most film versions cut or adapt a great deal of the original book.

- This extract from a **screenplay** (the technical name for a film script which includes instructions about camera work) will help to start you off. Look carefully at the layout and read the notes at the bottom.

INT. C.U. OF SIR HENRY	159
CUT TO	
INT. C.U. OF BARRYMORE	160
BARRYMORE Nothing, sir.	
CUT TO	
INT. C.U. OF BARRYMORE'S SHAKING HAND, HOLDING THE CANDLE	161
It was the window, sir.	
CUT TO	
INT. C.S. OF WATSON AND SIR HENRY, WATCHING BARRYMORE CLOSELY.	162
I go round at night	
CUT TO	
INT. L.S. OF BARRYMORE, FRAMED AGAINST THE WINDOW	163
to see that they are fastened.	

Layout

- Each shot is described as (i) either inside (INT.) or outside (EXT.); and (ii) close-up, long-shot, etc.
- The shot is written in capitals and underlined.
- The number of the shot is printed on the right.
- Dialogue is set out in the middle of the page, under the character's name.

Technique

- The montage – quick changes of shot – enables us to take in everybody's reaction
- The close-up of Barrymore's hand allows us to see how much he is shaking.
- After the close-ups and close-shot, we see Barrymore framed against the window – he looks lost and frightened.

Unit 10 Book, theatre, radio and cinema
Language of media and the moving image

Adapting a novel for different media

Here is the section from *The Hound of the Baskervilles* which follows the extract on page 63 of your book.

'What are you doing here, Barrymore?'

'Nothing, sir.' His agitation was so great that he could hardly speak, and the shadows sprang up and down from the shaking of his candle. 'It was the window, sir. I go round at night to see that they are fastened.'

'On the second floor?'

'Yes, sir, all the windows.'

'Look here, Barrymore,' said Sir Henry sternly, 'we have made up our minds to have the truth out of you, so it will save you the trouble to tell it sooner rather than later. Come now! No lies! What were you doing at that window?'

The fellow looked at us in a helpless way, and he wrung his hands together like one who is in the last extremity of doubt and misery.

'I was doing no harm, sir. I was holding a candle to the window.'

'And why were you holding a candle to the window?'

'Don't ask me, Sir Henry – don't ask me! I give you my word, sir, that it is not my secret, and that I cannot tell it. If it concerned no one but myself I would not try to keep it from you.'

A sudden idea occurred to me, and I took the candle from the window-sill where the butler had placed it.

'He must have been holding it up as a signal,' said I. 'Let us see if there is any answer.'

I held it up as he had done, and stared out into the darkness of the night. Vaguely I could discern the black bank of the trees and the lighter expanse of the moor, for the moon was behind the clouds. And then I gave a cry of exultation, for a tiny pin-point of yellow light had suddenly transfixed the dark veil, and glowed steadily in the centre of the black square framed by the window.

'There it is!' I cried.

Arthur Conan Doyle

Checking the language

11.1

> A **slogan** is a short, catchy phrase designed to stick in the memory.

Slogans can be used to get all sorts of messages across. They might try to persuade you that a product is something that everybody else wants, or that it's sexy or glamorous, or that it's the best product of its kind. To understand more about them, answer these questions in note form.

1. Which slogan has been chosen to finish off the magazine advertisement?

   Which of the following messages is the slogan trying to get across, in your opinion?

   That Clarks shoes are:
   - comfortable
   - the best you can buy
   - brilliantly designed
   - hard-wearing
   - fun
   - very unusual

   or a combination of two or more of these qualities?

2. The slogan of the television advertisement is spoken rather than written. What is it? How does it help to get the message across?

> **Montage** is the name given to the skill of joining moving-image shots together to achieve a particular effect.

When you use a montage of several shots you can get a message across to the viewer which couldn't be conveyed by any one of the shots on its own. The montage in the first section of the Clarks television advertisement (the scene in the park) helps to get the message across that the man is really pleased with his shoes. We cut from a shot of the man lifting his foot, not kicking the ball back, to his smug expression.

3. A single shot of a student sitting at an exam desk doesn't get much of a message across. But look at this description of a piece of montage. Draw a frame for each shot. Then write down what story the whole sequence seems to be telling.

   Shot 1: Student looks in horror at the exam paper.

   Shot 2: Cut to a shot of the clock, showing 9.30.

   Shot 3: Cut back to the student (sweating and sucking their pen).

   Shot 4: Back to the clock, now showing 11.30.

   Shot 5: Back to the student (now slumped over the desk). A voice is heard calling out 'Time's up. Put your pens down.'

Further language practice 11.2

> All advertisements are aimed at a particular audience. They are known as the **target group**.

For example, television advertisements for computer games are aimed mainly at boys up to 15 years old; most shampoo advertisements are aimed at women in the 16–35 age group. When a new advertisement is being planned, the makers have to ask themselves at least two questions:

Which gender are we aiming at?

male	female	both

Which age group are we aiming at?

Up to 15	16–24	25–35	36–55	Over 55

1 Which target groups are the following products likely to be aimed at? For each one, write down (a) the gender group; and (b) the age group.

Products	Gender group	Age group
Washing powders		
Expensive cars		
Do-it-yourself equipment		
Mobile phones		
Pop albums		
Make-up		

2 Fill in this chart with your own products and their target groups.

Products	Gender group	Age group

© Cambridge University Press 2001

Homework and revision

11.3

The differences between print-media texts and moving-image texts mean that each medium has its own built-in advantages and disadvantages. There are things you can do in one medium that you can't do in the other.

1 Each of the statements below describes an advantage of either (a) print-media texts, or (b) moving-image texts. Place each statement in one of the two columns of the table below. Two examples have been filled in to start you off.

Some advantages of either (a) print-media texts or (b) moving-image texts are:
- They are cheap to produce.
- They can use moving images and sound.
- They are easy to copy.
- You can read or scan them at whatever speed you like.
- They can let you hear a speaker's tone of voice.
- A large group of people can experience them at the same time.
- You can look at any section as often as you like.
- You can look away and, when you look back, the page is still there.
- The page is usually numbered so that you can find it again easily.
- They can use music, sound effects and silence.

Some advantages of print-media texts (Anything printed on a page, e.g. newspapers, magazines, books, your own writing, advertisements, most web-pages.)	Some advantages of moving-image texts (Anything on a screen which has duration, e.g. films, television programmes and personal moving-image web-pages.)
• *They are cheap to produce.*	• *They can use moving images and sound.*

These are some of the disadvantages of moving-image texts:
- You can't 'read' a moving-image text at any speed you like.
- You can look at different things on the screen – but only so long as they stay there.
- If you look away and look back again, the image is likely to have changed.
- It's harder to find a particular moment again (you have to rewind or fast-forward your video).
- In a cinema, you are not able to rewind or fast-forward.
- You need expensive technology to make moving-image texts such as films.
- It is much harder to make copies.

2 List some disadvantages of print-media texts.

Comparing print-media and television advertising

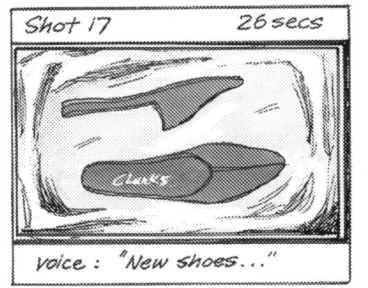

11.4

Farandole £35. From Clarks, K Shoes and other top shoe shops. Enquiry line 08705 785886.

How to get your new shoes noticed.

Wear convict trousers. — Gorton £59
Set up a display in your window. — Fiala £59
Walk on your hands. — Scene £35

Clarks
Act your shoe size, not your age.

Shot 7 — 07 secs
Shot 11 — 19 secs
Shot 15 — 21 secs
Shot 17 — 26 secs — voice: "New shoes..."
Shot 18 — 27 secs — voice: "Aaaah!"

Unit 11 Ways of selling
Language of media and the moving image

Assessing your own work

Comparing texts

When teachers and examiners mark and assess your work, they sometimes give it a level. Look carefully at this chart and decide at which level you would place yourself. First judge your work against the criteria in the **Word** column, then **Sentence** and finally **Text**.

- Your teacher might also use this chart.
- The language skills that you have been practising are highlighted in **bold**.
- In the box marked **Targets**, make a note of the language skills which you need to revise, or the new skills that you now want to develop.

Learning about the language of comparing texts

	WORD	✓	SENTENCE	✓	TEXT	✓
Level 3 Reading					You can understand the main points in a text.	
Level 3 Writing	You choose a variety of interesting words. You spell most common words correctly.		Most of your sentences are correctly put together, following the rules of grammar. You use capital letters, full stops and question marks correctly to show the beginnings and ends of sentences.		Your writing is well organised and clear. It shows that you have thought about who is going to read it.	
Level 4 Reading					You can pick out the most important ideas in a text. You refer back to the text when explaining your views. You can find and use ideas and information.	
Level 4 Writing	You use words for particular effects. You spell all common words correctly.		You use punctuation within sentences (full stops, capital letters and question marks). You are beginning to use complex sentences.		Your writing is lively and thoughtful. You develop your ideas in interesting ways.	
Level 5 Reading					You can select sentences and information to support your views. You can retrieve and collect together information from a range of different sources.	
Level 5 Writing	You choose imaginative vocabulary and use words precisely. You usually spell complex, regular words correctly.		You use a range of punctuation correctly (including apostrophes and inverted commas). You use simple and complex sentences confidently.		You can judge when to use a formal style. You organise sentences into paragraphs. You can judge when to use the first person or the third person. You take into account who is going to read your writing.	
Level 6 Reading	You understand **specialist language to do with media scripts.**		You understand features such as **sequencing**, **framing** and **soundtrack** in moving-image texts.		You understand **how meaning is conveyed** in texts that include print, images and sounds.	
Level 6 Writing	You vary your vocabulary to create particular effects. You usually spell complex, irregular words correctly.		You use punctuation such as semi-colons to make your meaning clear. You use a range of sentence structures to achieve different effects.		Your writing captures the reader's interest and holds it. You are able to **write in different forms** (such as **playscript** and **screenplay**).	
Level 7 Reading					You understand the idea of **target groups in advertising**. You understand the ways in which the **nature and purpose of media products influences the content and meaning.**	
Level 7 Writing	Your spelling is nearly always correct. You choose vocabulary with great care and accuracy.		You select sentence structures to suit the ideas you want to convey.		You can judge when to use **particular forms** and styles of writing, including the **appropriate layout for different media scripts**. You understand the **strengths and weaknesses of print-media and moving-image texts.**	

Targets

Glossary

Adjective

A word which describes somebody or something. It gives more information about a noun or pronoun, e.g. *the **latest dramatic** episode* (Unit 1, p. 1).

Adjectival phrase

A group of words which does the same job as an adjective, e.g. ***ex-England football captain** Gary Lineker* (Unit 1, pp. 10–11).

Angles

Camera shots from different directions and different heights, e.g. *from below, looking up* or *from the side* (Unit 9, p. 58).

Caption

A short piece of writing which explains, or comments on, an image, e.g. *Wear convict trousers* (Unit 11, p. 77).

Casting

The choice of actors to play particular parts, e.g. *Robert de Niro to play Frankenstein's monster* (Unit 9, p. 59).

Colloquial language

Vocabulary and expressions which are closer to everyday, informal speech, e.g. *He **bawled** desperately to **cops** to help him* (Unit 3, p. 22).

Copy

The written text in an advertisement. The main block of copy is known as the **body copy** (Unit 4, p. 29).

Cutting

The skill of changing from one film shot to another (Unit 8, p. 53).

Duration

Moving-image texts have **duration**. Film-makers have to think about how much time to give to each shot (Unit 11, p. 77).

Editing

The skill of selecting, and joining, camera shots (Unit 7, p. 47).

Emotive words

Words which have a particular effect on our feelings and emotions, e.g. ***Warm, white** beaches are **lapped** by **clear blue** seas* (Unit 4, p. 28).

Frame

A single image on a strip of film (Unit 7, p. 46).

Framing

The skill of placing people or objects in different positions within the edges of the film frame to get particular effects (Unit 8, pp. 52–53; Unit 9, p. 58; Unit 10, p. 69).

Genres

The different kinds of books and films with their own special features, e.g. *horror, western, science fiction* (Unit 6, p. 41; Unit 8, p. 53).

Graphics

The art of putting images and lettering together for a special effect (Unit 5, p. 35).

Homophones

Words which sound the same, but have different spellings and meanings, e.g. *here* and *hear* (Unit 5, p. 34).

Image

A picture used by an advertiser to achieve a particular effect (Unit 4, p. 29; Unit 11, p. 76).

Imperative sentences
Sentences which tell you or ask you to do something, e.g. *Keep out! Have a sandwich.* (Unit 5, p. 34).

Interpretation
Somebody's idea of what a book, play or film means. **Interpreting** a script means performing it in certain ways and making the audience notice particular things or respond in particular ways (Unit 9, p. 59).

Intro
The opening paragraph or sentence of a newspaper article, e.g. *Britain's `flu outbreak is getting worse* (Unit 2, p. 17).

Jargon
Special vocabulary used by particular groups of people, e.g. *body copy* (Unit 4, p. 29).

Location
The place where a scene is filmed (Unit 9, p. 59; Unit 10, p. 68).

Logo
A special symbol which represents a large organisation such as a business, a charity or a college, e.g. the penguin on Penguin books (Unit 5, p. 35).

Media
Sources of information, advertising and entertainment, such as the press, television, cinema or the Internet. **Print media** include newspapers, magazines and posters. **Moving-image media** include films, television and video. (*Media* is plural – we talk of one *medium*.) (Unit 4, p. 29, Unit 6, p. 40)

Montage
The skill of joining moving image shots together to achieve a particular effect (Unit 8, p. 53; Unit 10, p. 69).

Paragraph
A block of sentences linked by one overall idea or topic, e.g. the first paragraph of *Stop Him!* which introduces the story (Unit 3, p. 23).

Parody
A comedy film or book which mocks the typical features of a particular genre, e.g. *Red Dwarf*, which is a parody of science fiction (Unit 6, p. 41).

Props
Short for *properties* – all the hand-held objects used in a play or film (Unit 9, p. 59).

Pun
The use of two words with different meanings but similar sounds for a humorous effect, e.g. **Hole** *lotta trouble* (Unit 1, p. 10, Unit 5, p. 34).

Quotes
Someone's exact words, e.g. *Matthew Lazzara said:* **'This is a very big iceberg.'** (Unit 2, p. 16).

Register
The style of language we choose, to suit a particular situation or a certain kind of subject matter. The iceberg article (pp. 14–15) is in a formal register; the *Stop Him!* article (pp. 20–21) is mainly in an informal register (Unit 3, p. 22).

Rhyme
The effect achieved by using words with the same, or similar, sounds, e.g. *Down* **under blunder** (Unit 1, p. 10).